The Time of

The Time of Your Life

Sheila Dainow

BOXTREE

First published in Great Britain in 1994 by Boxtree Limited,
Broadwall House, 21 Broadwall, London SE1 9PL

10 9 8 7 6 5 4 3 2 1

ISBN 1 85283 535 4

Cover design by Robert Updegraff
Cover photographs © Lupe Cunha

Typeset by SX Composing Limited
Printed and bound in Great Britain
by Cox & Wyman Ltd, Reading, Berkshire

A CIP catalogue entry for this book is available from the
British Library

To Liesl Silverstone, Sister-in-Spirit

Contents

Acknowledgements

It is always a pleasure to be able to give public thanks to those people whose support I have appreciated while writing this book.

Firstly, to clients and students from whom I learn all the time. Many of the exercises and lines of thought have developed as a result of my work with them.

I remain grateful to Carole Blake, a very 'Special Agent!'

And personally, as always to Cyril, Jo and Alisa for their constant love, support and gentle (well, sometimes) criticism. To spend my time with them has been, is and will continue to be a pleasure.

Introduction

'Then do not squander time, for that's the stuff life is made of'
(*Benjamin Franklin 1706-90*).

Thoughts about time

Are you feeling overwhelmed by the demands made on you by
other people? Are the pressures made on you by your job getting
you down? Perhaps you are feeling life is passing you by or that it
could be more satisfying than it is. You may be at the time of life
when you want to be sure that the years remaining to you are
well-spent. Or at a stage where there is so much time that you
don't know where to start. Maybe you want to make changes in
your life but you feel that time and the clock are against you. Perhaps the title of the book started you thinking about how you are
spending the time of your life – and that you would like to make
some changes.

This book may be what you have been looking for. It offers you
the opportunity to explore how you are spending your life at the
moment and gives practical ideas for changing.

Time has fascinated people throughout the ages. It is the one
thing that we are all given in equal amounts. Whether rich or
poor, we all have the same number of minutes in an hour, hours
in a day and days in a year. Other resources are not so equally
distributed and it's easy to feel that if you don't have a lot of
money or talent it is not possible to increase satisfaction and
accomplish achievement in the time you have. However, in reading this book, you may discover that it is possible to make some
changes in how you are approaching life at the moment which
don't require money or other material resources. These changes

1

are designed to help you feel more in control so that you are using your time to the best advantage for you and those around you.

Despite the fact that we all have it, time is very difficult to define. The Benjamin Franklin quote implies that your time is your life. So, if you waste your time, you waste your life. The way we think about time is often distorted; for instance whereas we sometimes feel with the Roman poet Virgil, 'irretrievable time is flying' at other times Keats' heartfelt 'Oh aching time! O moments as big as years!' is more appropriate. Of course, time actually neither flies or drags – it moves at a predetermined rate. Another error in our thinking is to believe we can 'save' time. We cannot really do that – we cannot put the hours or minutes into a bank and collect interest on them. We cannot 'make up' time which we feel is wasted – once it is gone it is irretrievable.

The first most important matter with regard to thinking about how you are spending the time of your life is to decide who is in control – you or time. You have many resources, apart from time, to help you live your life – your state of health, your personality, your material possessions, your talents and so on. All of these, except time, can be in some way manipulated and controlled by you if you choose. For instance, you can change your lifestyle to improve your health, embark on psychotherapy to understand and change aspects of your personality, acquire or sell personal belongings, develop your skill and talents. But time is unique. It is finite. You cannot have any more or less of it than there is. You can have 60 seconds for each minute; 60 minutes for each day; 24 hours each day; 365 days each year. No discounts; no inflation; no hidden supply. Exploring how to manage this resource so that you are getting the best out of life is the purpose of this book.

However, as we have already seen, time itself is not open to change. You cannot choose *whether* to spend it, only *how*. Managing *time* really means managing *yourself* in relation to the time you have.

If you are wondering whether it is possible for you to take more control over your time and if that will help you be more in control of your life – the answer is *YES*! You can – if you have confidence in yourself, if you have the information you need, if you know how to use the information and if you are willing to risk change.

The world of business has acknowledged the value of this idea for many years; managers attend time management courses, experts in time and motion are called in to analyse how the work is being done.

This book will give you, firstly, an opportunity to consider how your present attitude to time helps or hinders you. You will also have a chance to analyse how you are spending your time at the moment with a view to deciding how to change things. Then we will look at various practical options open to you. If you are willing to take the time to explore your present thinking and do those exercises which seem most appropriate to your particular situation, you will be able to use your time to gain more benefit for yourself – and those around you.

1

THE DESTRUCTIVE CIRCLE

Do you ever:

- Wonder what you have been doing with your life?
- Wish you could change your direction in life?
- Wonder how you could get more of what you want out of life?
- Look at the clock and wonder where the time went?
- Find your life tedious?
- Experience life as a struggle?
- Feel out of control of your life?

You are probably reading this book because you can answer 'yes' to one or more of the above questions. This could be your first step towards succeeding in the changes you want. Not because this book has all the answers but because picking up a book is a positive action – and positive action is what will help you change.

This first chapter will help you understand more about why it can be so difficult to effect the changes which could make all the difference between feeling happy and fulfilled or miserable and dissatisfied with life.

Stress is an important factor. Over the past few years there has been a growing awareness of the toll that stress can take. Much is being written about links between many illnesses and the stress of contemporary life; stress is often cited as a major factor in family breakdown; some people are driven to rely on drugs or drink in order to get them through. Stress is certainly one of the demons we have to contend with in modern-day existence.

Living in a stressful world is bound to create tension. Actually, this is not altogether a bad thing for we all have a level of pressure which is right for us. It is only when pressure on us is either higher or lower than this ideal level that we experience stress. The idea of a life where few unreasonable or difficult demands are made on you may seem like a wonderful fantasy, but here is just a word of warning. When demands are few and pressure is low, most people respond by becoming less energetic and feeling less alive, so far from being a pleasurable experience, a life with too little pressure can leave you feeling bored with little to look forward to. In fact, avoiding stress does not mean eliminating pressure, even if it could be done. To remove all pressure is stressful – you just have to think of prisoners in solitary confinement to realize that. A less dramatic example is the effect on some people when they retire from work – an event they may have looked forward to for years. If you've ever had a job with not enough to do you will know just how tedious clockwatching can be.

As the level of pressure increases, so does your level of alertness and attention. You respond by feeling stimulated, lively and ready for life. At this point the pressure level is right for you. The time seems to match the amount you are trying to achieve and you feel on top of life.

If the pressure level continues to rise, feelings of tension increase and this is when you begin to feel you are struggling to cope. Time begins to slip away. Minutes, hours, sometimes whole days seem to fly without you achieving anything of worth. You may, by using a great deal of energy, appear to be coping well so that other people won't be aware of the struggle. But this attempt to keep the appearance of control itself adds to the stress.

Stress: The Fight or Flight Response

Why is stress a problem? For the answer to this we have to go back to prehistoric times. One way of describing our problem is that we have developed minds capable of creating the Space Age and bodies which are still in the Stone Age. Imagine you are living the life of one of your Stone Age ancestors. You are sitting quite comfortably in your cave and suddenly you see a huge dinosaur's shadow on the cave wall. You look outside and there is an enormous prehistoric beast sniffing around the entrance. What do you do? Well, you only really have two options – you can jump past the beast and run for safety or you can stand your ground and fight. You have to make up your mind quickly, otherwise you won't have a mind to make up at all. The mechanism which developed to enable us to get out of that kind of trouble is still part of our make-up today. It is called the fight or flight response and is part of our physiological programming. Although we don't have to deal with prehistoric animals, we do have modern-day 'monsters' to face and each time we perceive a threat we respond in the way we always have – fight or flight.

Consider two examples of modern 'monsters':

1 You are in a heated argument with your partner and something is said which indicates he or she has completely misunderstood you. You may notice that your breathing speeds up, you feel angry and frustrated; maybe you clench your fists and glare at your partner. You may be tempted to strike him or her, but you know this is not wise and manage to contain your spontaneous response.

2 You open a letter from your bank manager which tells you that you are severely overdrawn. As far as you knew, you were well in credit. You might come out in a cold sweat; perhaps you feel anxious and want to run away; your mind seems paralysed so that you can't think clearly about your accounts.

Although these situations have triggered different feelings, in the first case anger and in the second fear, they are both emotional labels describing the response of fight or flight.

This response is activated by our brain which alerts our body to the need for action. A chain of events starts in the central nervous system to equip us with what we need in order to fight or flee the threat. A variety of hormones are secreted, including adrenalin which increases the level of arousal in our body. It is as if the body is preparing itself for war, ready to deal with the threat. Fuel has to reach the muscles which need to be strengthened for the coming activity. The bloodstream is the body's main transport system so you may notice your heart beating faster when you are in a tight spot, as the blood is pumped round more quickly then usual. The blood is directed away from the skin and internal organs and rushed to where the body thinks it is needed. The supply of oxygen needed to burn glucose, the main body fuel, is increased and so breathing becomes more rapid and intense.

The digestive system slows down because the body cannot cope with the normal processes of digestion while all this other activity is going on. You begin to sweat because the body needs to cool down the heat generated.

This has taken you a few seconds to read, but it actually happens in a flash. It is our experience of this process which we have labelled with various names – fear, anger, excitement, etc. The name we give it depends on the particular experience we are having.

It is a problem because, although it was a brilliant way of dealing with Stone Age monsters which only understood fight or flight, it is not so effective in dealing with our Space Age mammoths. Most of the time, we cannot run away or strike someone. We have to contain our anger or fear and face the threat in some other way.

> *Exercise: Before you read any further take a moment or two to list the 'monsters' you face in your day-to-day life. Think about your reaction to each one – what are your thoughts, feelings and behaviour when you are facing them.*

Some very common modern-day pressures which might feature in your list:

- Losing your job;
- Household bills which cannot be paid;
- Working with an 'awkward' boss;
- Cramped living conditions;
- Arguments with your children;
- Trains which don't arrive on time;

- Pollution in the environment;
- Living with someone who doesn't understand your needs;
- Being caught in a traffic jam;
- Uncertainty about the future;
- Vandalism;
- Illness of close friends or relatives.

The long-term danger with this situation is that because we generally do not take the action for which our bodies have prepared when we face our modern monsters, our body remains constantly in a state of arousal. The heart rate, which increased to get more blood to the muscles, can be permanently raised, resulting in high blood pressure. The rapid breathing to increase the supply of oxygen can lead to respiratory problems or hyperventilation. Muscle tension, which is necessary for running or hitting someone, can lead to pain in the neck, shoulders and back. Sweating changes the resistance of the surface of the skin and can make it susceptible to rashes and skin problems.

Combating Stress

Don't despair – it's not all gloom and doom! The trouble with this kind of exploration is that the more detailed we get the more gloomy the picture seems. Of course you won't have problems in all these areas. Although maybe you have become aware that when you are under pressure, it tends to make itself felt in a particular place. Perhaps you get a headache or a backache or suffer from anxiety attacks. Your increasing awareness is one of your greatest weapons in alleviating the symptoms you experience. After all, an enemy you can see and understand is much easier to fight than one who is invisible and unpredictable. We've all heard the saying, 'the strongest chain will break at its weakest link'. Knowing your own weak link is important because you can go about strengthening it. Where your particular weak point is located depends on at least two factors: the nature of your lifestyle and those traits you inherited at birth. Although you cannot do much about your genetic inheritance, you can certainly take control of your lifestyle. You may as a result of this book decide on some changes which will reduce the amount of stress in your life.

The fight or flight response was developed to solve a problem –

how to remain alive in a world full of physical danger. It certainly solved that problem to some extent, but it also created the problems of the destructive circle. Our brain perceives a threat and sends a message to the body to prepare for action. The body prepares for action by stimulating itself. The threat is dealt with but the body is still in a stressed state as a result of undischarged energy, so the brain perceives a threat . . . and so on. The circle is sometimes unintentionally strengthened by us as we look for ways of reducing the pressure – smoking, eating sweets, drinking coffee, alcohol and so on. All of these in some way put extra stress on our bodies as they stimulate or calm us down. Extricating yourself from this destructive circle will be an important move towards getting more out of life. When you are under too much pressure you are often in so much of a rush that you fail to notice how stressed you are becoming. The earlier you notice, the better position you are in to take corrective action. You won't have to wait until the symptoms are so severe that you have no choice.

It is reassuring to know that there is no such thing as a normal response to pressure; each of us responds to stress in our own particular way and sometimes, as we have seen, we actually increase the amount of stress we have to contend with by our response. Try thinking about yourself as a system with each individual part linked to and affected by every other part. Just like any other system, if one element is malfunctioning the rest will be affected. When you are trying to identify your stress responses look for any pattern of change in thought, feeling and behaviour you experience when you are stressed. As stress increases, your whole system responds and any part of the system can show a reaction.

One way of describing our personality as a system is by identifying the following four main components, which although separate are inextricably linked to each other:

> *Thoughts:* Our thoughts help us to make sense of the world. If our level of stress increases, the way we think changes. We tend to slip into habitual or conditioned ways of thinking about ourselves or the world in general. We may find it hard to concentrate, we put things off, become obsessed by details, find it hard to think clearly and logically.

9

Feelings: The way we feel can also change under stress so that we experience emotions like panic or elation; depression or guilt. If our emotional response is appropriate to the situation there is no problem. After all, if you are walking down a strange dark street and hear footsteps coming up behind you it would be appropriate to feel a twinge of fear or apprehension. However, sometimes our response is not appropriate; it might be too intense or not strong enough. Preparing to speak at a meeting might induce great feelings of fear and yet when considered logically, nothing can actually happen which merits the paralysing effect that some people experience in such situations. Sometimes stress has the effect of distorting our emotional response so that we show anger when we are afraid; or we cry when we are happy. Just think about the response of a parent who has been waiting up for a child who comes back much later than expected. The parent is desperately worried that something terrible has happened to their son or daughter and feels intense fear. But the moment he or she arrives, the parent explodes with anger.

Behaviour: What we actually do is often very influenced by stress. Someone who is usually quiet and polite might find themselves shouting. Speech can become confused; levels of agitation can increase. A person can become hostile and angry or, on the other hand, passive and withdrawn.

Physical response: Our bodies can also change how they function during times of stress. Bouts of indigestion and headaches are not uncommon. Muscular tension can increase; we can feel sweaty or tremble with cold.

These four elements – thoughts, feelings, behaviour and physical response are closely connected. For instance, if your body is out of sorts, your thoughts, feelings and behaviour will be affected. Experiencing strong feelings will affect how you think and what you do and so on.

Exercise: How does pressure affect you? The following questionnaire will help you understand more about your own response to pressure.

1 Was there a time in your life when life presented few demands or challenges? If so, during this time:

- How well were you able to think, concentrate, plan, etc.? What feelings do you remember having?

- What kind of things did you do? Were there any familiar patterns of behaviour you engaged in at the time?

- Was there any change in your state of health or any effect on your body at this time?

2 Now choose a time in your life when the pressure level seemed just right for you; a time when you felt you were functioning at your best. Use your memory of this time to answer the above questions again.

3 Lastly, take a time when you were experiencing a high level of pressure; when life seemed like a struggle and full of tension. Once again answer the four questions.

Notice any differences in how you tend to think, feel and act in response to different levels of pressure. This exercise will raise your awareness as to how your system responds to the different stress levels you experience. You may want to repeat the exercise about different life events so that you get an idea of the range of responses you have. You can ask those who know you for their opinions – very often others notice changes in us of which we are unaware.

An Early Survival Guide

Let's think about how this all began. When you were young you needed to make sense of the world; adults like your parents and teachers gave you guidance in many ways about how to behave. Some things they told you directly; they rewarded or punished you for certain behaviour; they encouraged you to copy how they behaved. One way or another you realized certain behaviour as acceptable and other behaviour wasn't. Gradually you began to make decisions about the nature of the world and what kind of person you were. These decisions make up the core of your beliefs about the world, about how you and others should behave and think, about what is right and wrong. This process is going on all the time as we go through life, gaining more and more information and experience, but these early decisions remain very influential. This process has been likened to having an internal tape recorder which is activated when we are born and then records every message we receive. Unlike a real tape-recorder, however, it does not record new material over old. This one works so that all new messages have to be screened through the already existing ones. In this way, very early decisions are always there – and come to the fore when we are under stress.

For example, as a result of finding yourself in your particular family you will have reached certain conclusions about family life. These will result from what you were told, what you observed and what you experienced. From your early perceptions you will have built up an intricate picture of 'family life' and this will affect your expectations and beliefs.

These decisions you made early on felt like 'facts' so you could tell yourself 'this is how the world is and this is the best way for me to survive in it.' You were in fact writing a survival guide made up of the strategies which seemed to meet your needs at the time. The trouble is that you very rarely get a chance to review this guide, which was created such a long time ago with so little information. When you made those decisions you were very small with very little power in a world ruled by 'big' people. Now you are an adult, just as big as everyone else, with the ability to think and evaluate. It is interesting that many people report that when they are under stress, they actually feel younger and smaller.

It is important, when the pressure is on, to know whether your response is being influenced by past decisions. It is very useful to take a moment to listen to what you're telling yourself. Here are five very typical messages people give themselves – common parts of the survival guide for many people. This particular idea comes from Claude Steiner, one of the originators of Trans-actional Analysis, a set of theories which sets out to explain how people develop their personality. Steiner described these five patterns of response to stress:

'I've got to get it right' This message comes from an early perception that the way to survive and to be acceptable is to succeed, to do really well, to be perfect. The idea would come from parental messages like 'don't make a mistake'; 'don't take risks'; 'being first is more valuable than being second'. The effect of this message is not to be satisfied with anything that is less than perfect; under stress this becomes an obsession. In your more rational moments you will realize that many things in life can never be perfect, but under stress you will refer to the survival guide! And that will instruct you to put all your energy into keeping everything and everybody under control so that you can get it right.

When the pressure is on, time will be stolen by this idea because you will get tied up with trying to get every single detail right; checking and rechecking. It becomes difficult to know when your achievement is good enough so that you can move on to the next thing.

'I must keep everyone happy' This idea comes from the realization that you have to please everybody to be acceptable yourself. It leads you to believe that you should behave in ways which will suit other people rather than yourself. It comes from early messages like 'don't be assertive'; 'you are not important'; 'don't be different'; 'don't say 'no''. The effect is that you feel you have to placate people whom you might prefer to ignore or confront; that you deny your own needs in order to fulfil others' demands; that you find it difficult to say 'no' when it might be wiser for you to do so. You find yourself spending a lot of time trying to guess what other people want so that you can please them.

'I must be brave' This message is about hiding your fears and feelings so that you appear strong. It comes from the early communication 'don't show your feelings'; 'don't give in'; 'it is weak to ask for help'. It means that you will deny yourself help from other people and keep struggling rather than risk appearing weak by asking for help.

'I've got to keep on trying' This is the idea that the amount of effort you put into doing things is as, or even more, important than the result. The main thing to remember with regard to this exhortation to try hard is that *trying* is not the same thing as

13

doing. Very often, parents in their attempts to be kind and loving to children say something like 'You know, it isn't necessary to keep worrying about getting to the top and beating everyone else; all we want from you is that you try your hardest.' On the surface, there doesn't seem to be much wrong with this message, but the child may hear 'We will only love you as long as you keep trying.' The problem here is that the survival guide doesn't include the information that you will continue to be loved when you have finished the task. If so, you might unconsciously set things up so that you never actually finish much. Examples might be procrastination (after all, if you don't start, you can't finish!), taking on too much so that there is always something left undone, tiring yourself out by energetic trying so that no energy is left for finishing.

'I must do it quickly' This is the message that speed counts. Do this fast and move on to the next task is the survival message. Adults do often seem to be hurrying children up – after all, since they are bigger they move faster and sometimes find it frustrating to move at what seems like a snail's pace. You might very early on get the idea that you can only survive if you don't take too long or waste time. So under stress you will find yourself in a frenetic whirl of activity in which you might miss things or make mistakes.

Of course, there isn't anything wrong with these messages – in fact taken sensibly they are a good guide to survival in our kind of society where perfection, pleasing others, strength, persistence and speed are highly valued. In trying to pass these values on to us, our parents and teachers were doing their best to help us develop in such a way that we would be happy and keep healthy. The problem arises because when we were very young we were not able to understand that these messages were intended as guidelines rather than strict instructions. When we are under stress our mind moves into familiar thinking patterns and we once again hear the instructions: 'You *must* get it right/please everyone/keep strong/keep trying/be speedy.' When the pressure is on one or a mixture of these messages overrides what is realistic and appropriate in the particular situation. It will seem like a matter of life and death that you obey the commands. They, in

14

themselves, are a cause of pressure and so the destructive circle revolves again.

If you do identify with any or all of the messages, it is important for you to remember that although they seem to be inscribed on tablets of stone, they are not. You were not born believing them. They are your internalized version of what you learned and decided years ago. They might have been invaluable rules at the time but they may now be out-of-date. If you do still find yourself acting on them without question you need to review whether this is the wisest option.

> *Exercise: Here is a quiz to help you identify which are the strongest messages in your own personal survival guide.*
> *Tick Yes, Sometimes or No column (Y/S/N) for each question.*

	Y	S	N
1. Do you like to explain things in detail?			
2. Is it important for you to be right?			
3. Would you notice a blemish however small, e.g. a typing error or button missing?			
4. Do you hate interruptions?			
5. Do you have high standards which you criticise yourself and others for not meeting?			
6. Is it important to you to be liked?			
7. Do you find yourself doing things for other people for which they haven't asked, or that you don't really want to do?			
8. Are you easily persuaded?			
9. Do you try to avoid conflict?			
10. Do you like to feel you fit in?			
11. Do you hide your feelings?			

	Y	S	N
12. Do a lot of people seem to depend on you?			
13. Do you prefer not to ask for help?			
14. Do you keep going without noticing how tired or hungry you might be?			
15. Do you prefer to do things on your own?			
16. Do you often find yourself the 'odd one out'?			
17. Are there many things you intend to start but have put off?			
18. Do you have a tendency to start things and not finish them?			
19. If you are engaged in something which is not working, do you hate to 'give in'?			
20. Do you often find yourself going round in circles, feeling stuck but not being able to let go the problem?			
21. Do you finish other people's sentences for them?			
22. Do you hate to waste time?			
23. Do you find yourself wishing other people would 'get on with it' rather than just 'talk about it'?			
24. Are you often late for appointments, because you were too busy to leave on time?			
25. Are you impatient with other people who seem slow?			

To score: Score 3 points for a yes, 2 points for sometimes and 0 points for no. The quiz is arranged in five sections each relating to a different message. Add up your score separately for questions 1–5 (The 'You must get it right' message): 6–10 ('You've got to keep everyone pleased'); 11–15 ('You must be brave'); 16–20 ('Keep on trying'); 21–25 ('You must do it quickly'). Notice which sections have the highest score; these are indications of the instructions you give yourself when you are stressed. You will also see that sometimes you are giving yourself conflicting messages. You might have a high score in section 1–5 ('You've got to get it right') and in section 21–25 ('You've got to do it quickly'). As you speed up, it's likely you will make mistakes – or create blemishes on the perfection you are trying to achieve. So your stress increases . . .!

Each of the behaviour types carries benefits and costs and each affects how we use time. By becoming familiar with your own response, you can decide to capitalize on the benefits and reduce the costs so that your time is as well used as possible.

'You must get it right':   This is the instruction which often leads to success and achievement. If, from an early age, you learnt to be logical and use your understanding to get things right, this is what you will be doing now. Being successful and good at what you do is very satisfying. It becomes a problem when, under stress, getting it right becomes getting it 'perfect'. Trying to get the world perfect will inevitably lead to great frustration, since there doesn't seem to be any coherent idea as to what perfection should be. It would be more productive and less stressful to think about what would be good enough and then to identify the options open to you for achieving that.

If your score was high for the last category, try this:

> *Exercise: Make a list of all the things you are trying to get right at the moment. There will probably be quite small personal things and larger matters to do with the greater society. Now go through the list carefully and rate them in order of importance to you. Then take each one and decide what result would be good enough for you to feel you had achieved a resonable level of success. Then list what options for action are open to you for each item. Notice any tendency you have to set too high targets for yourself. Check all the time that what you are aiming for is reasonable, bearing in mind*

the resources available to you. Look at this list from time to time so that you can check whether you are keeping on a rational track or are wrestling with trying to change something in an irrational way.

'You must keep everyone happy': The great advantage of having had this early message is that you develop a good ability to get on with people. Pleasing and being pleased by people can make life very enriching. Positive contact with people helps us to grow and develop. Responding to the early understanding that pleasing people is productive helps to develop very good nurturing abilities. Again the problems arise when keeping people happy overrides any other consideration. There are times when, for instance, bringing a conflict out into the open will be more therapeutic for the people involved than trying to smooth it over. Whenever you find yourself thinking about how you can keep everyone pleased in a stressful situation, ask yourself, 'What are my needs now? What are the needs of the other people? How can I help myself and others?' The aim is not to change things so that you selfishly only consider yourself but to take your needs into consideration together with other people's. Doing this helps you to keep a better balance and saves you from feeling taken for granted or discounted.

If you had a high score for this category, try this exercise:

Exercise: Many groups have created a Bill of Rights for themselves. Write down your ideas for a Bill of Rights. It might include items like, 'the right to privacy'; 'the right to be heard'; 'the right to say 'no'. List all the things that people have a right to expect and that you would be willing to give them. Now rewrite the list as a Bill of Rights for you – don't leave out or change anything.

'You must be brave' is encouragement to stay strong and carry on without giving in to weakness. This decision brings with it admirable qualities of steadfastness and stoicism and great dependability. Strength of will is a great asset and one which will carry you through many difficult times. It becomes a liability when the need to be strong leaves you without any way of expressing your needs and feelings. Here is an exercise if you would like to lessen the disadvantages of this pattern:

> *Exercise: Write the words 'I want' in a column down one side of a sheet of paper. Then complete the sentences listing all the personal wants you can identify. Think about how you could begin to ask for some of these wants from the people around you.*

'Keep on trying': The great advantage of this message is that it encourages enthusiasm to try to achieve and the ability to persist with something. Under stress, the pattern which often develops around this message is one of leaving things unfinished. You will remember that the unconscious logic is that once something is finished, love and attention will be withdrawn. Reducing the personal costs of this message means being very careful about planning your time. Make a point of reading chapter 5 which focuses on how to plan so that you do achieve your goals and putting the various suggestions into action. Finish whatever you set out to do, even if you find the idea frightening. Get to know your own particular sabotage techniques like putting things off, setting unrealistic deadlines, losing or forgetting things and don't allow yourself to scuttle your efforts to change.

> *Exercise: Write down a list of all the things you have on the go at the moment. Decide which you want actually to finish and which you will let go. Now – finish those things you want to do!*

'You must do it quickly' has obvious advantages. Most of us are living complicated lives with several tasks to achieve. Responding to the DIQ instruction means that we are able to move quickly from one thing to another, often working on more than one element at a time. Anyone who has parented small children will know how useful it is to be able to hold a baby with one hand, prepare a meal with the other and answer the telephone all at the same time! Once again, when stress builds up, the costs outweigh the benefits. Instead of speedy competence, we move into frenzied chaos, rushing around and not achieving very much. To reduce the damage, you need to get into the habit of telling yourself to slow down. You will find many suggestions in Chapter 7, which will be of particular interest to you. Here is one exercise you can try now:

Exercise: Take an everyday action like opening a book, tying your shoe laces or putting on your watch and do it in slow motion. Take at least five minutes to finish the action. This will probably be difficult for you because you will keep thinking what a waste of time it is. Don't give in to any desire to finish it quickly, but do stay aware of your reaction. This would be a good activity for you to do at least once a day to remind yourself that you can slow down and to notice how much you may miss by hurrying as much as you do.

A Balancing Act

Another element to take into consideration is the way you balance time for this will affect how you are able to take control of your life. For instance, getting the home/work balance right can be very difficult. If you are busy and successful at work it may seem to you that work takes up an inordinate amount of time. But, work is not your whole life. What happens outside work and the amount of attention you pay to home, leisure and your social life are very important. Or you may be finding it difficult to maintain a balance between the attention you give to all the people in your life. You may find that you are devoting a great deal of time and energy to one over-demanding person at the expense of everyone else; you may feel that you are giving other people most of your attention, leaving very little energy for yourself. The following exercise will help you see how you are balancing your life at the moment.

Exercise: Make a list of all the ways you are using your time at the moment, making it as specific as possible. You can list the various people whom you spend time with as well as the tasks that you carry out. Now take a large sheet of paper and imagine that this represents your life at the moment. Using your list as a guide make a diagram or picture of your life including all the components you listed. Make the picture so that each item takes up the space it seems to in your life. When you have finished, some things to notice are: are there some items which take up much of the space?; are some items pushed out altogether?; are you happy with the picture?

This exercise might have started you thinking about ways in which you would like to change how you are using your time at the moment – later chapters will offer practical ways of making the changes you want.

2

CHECKING YOUR TIME
INVESTMENTS

The last chapter helped you step back and take a general look at your life overall – the next step is to consider in greater detail just how you are investing your time right now.

> *Exercise: This quiz is to help you identify danger signals warning you that you might be getting out of control of your time.*
>
> *Read through the list and use the scale to determine your score between 0 and 10 for each item on the list. Put your score in the blank next to each statement and then add them up to find out your total:*

Never	Sometimes	Frequently	Most of the Time	Always
0	1 2 3	4 5 6	7 8 9	10

_____ 1 *I take on lots of tasks because I feel that I'm the only one who can do them properly.*

_____ 2 *I'm dealing with crises all the time. I never get any time to do the really important things because everyday problems keep cropping up and I have to deal with them.*

____ 3 *I feel spread very thin. People are always asking me to do things for them and I don't like to refuse; I know I'm doing too much.*

____ 4 *I feel as if I'm always running to catch up with myself. I am very pressured and keep getting behind with what I want to achieve.*

____ 5 *I'm always working and never seem to get any time for myself to do what I really enjoy.*

____ 6 *Most of my time is taken up with doing things I don't really want to do.*

____ 7 *I feel guilty if I am pleasing myself and doing just what I want to do.*

____ 8 *I find it difficult to be definite about what to do and dither about deciding between the choices I have.*

____ 9 *When I do have spare time, I often feel too tired and listless to use it constructively.*

____ 10 *I constantly miss the deadlines I set myself.*

If you scored under 35 points, you've probably got things more or less under control, although it will be worth your while checking that you are not unwittingly increasing the pressure on yourself.

A score of 36–60 indicates that you would benefit greatly from reviewing your attitudes to time.

If your score is over 60, you're probably already feeling that you don't have enough time for all these exercises! It is likely that you are well established in the destructive circle described in Chapter 1, and if you were to slow down and allow yourself time to reflect, you would be able to identify changes that would actually give you more time and space.

It's interesting that while many people spend a lot of time analysing the intricate details of their financial investments, working

23

out the 'best buy' for their next purchase or discussing their financial future with their bank manager, few think of using this skill to assess their own lives.

> *Exercise: You will have heard the phrase 'Time is money'; imagine for the moment that it is true and that you have a time account just as you have financial accounts. Ask yourself:*
>
> - *What return are you getting for the time and energy you are using?*
> - *What is the 'best buy' in your life?*
> - *If you were a salesperson, how would you present the way you were managing your life at the moment?*
> - *How do you actually fill the hours of each day?*

How Safe is Your Time?

Imagine leaving one of your most valuable possessions – money, car, painting, silver, jewellery, etc. out in a public place, unlocked and unprotected in any way. I guess you probably wouldn't dream of doing this because it would seem like an invitation to the first thief who passed by. I wonder, though, how often you have allowed your *time* to be stolen. Time is like the other valuable resources you own; if you're not careful it can get lost or stolen.

Time stealers come in all shapes – little and large. Little ones include all those things that we allow to distract us from the things we have decided to do. Five minutes longer on the phone than we intended; agreeing to do 'a little job' for someone which we would rather have refused; spending too much time on something trying to get it just a bit more perfect, spending more time with someone in order to be thought of as 'nice' could all come into the category of time stealers.

There are larger time stealers, too, that can get between you and your life's goals. These are more to do with patterns of belief about yourself and others. For instance, a belief that you don't have the right to make decisions about your life or a certainty that other people are always more important will affect how you manage your time.

There are many examples of classic 'stolen-time scripts' created by certain systems of belief about time. Do you identify with any of these?

The Three Sisters or How to avoid the present moment: In Chekhov's play, the three sisters of the title live in a provincial town in North Russia which in their hearts they feel is not their home. In their hearts they inhabit Moscow. Much of their time is 'stolen' by looking back towards their Moscow childhood or longingly forward to the future when they plan to return. One character in the play says, 'The present is loathsome, but then when I think about the future – well, that's another story.' In some way or other, each character in the play refuses to live in the present. There are times for all of us, of course, when remembering the past and planning for the future are appropriate and enjoyable. This becomes a problem though if it is the way most of the time is spent. Practically speaking, the only time you actually have is the present. The past has gone, and although it can be thought about it cannot be lived again; the future is still to come and although we can fantasize about it we cannot control it.

Gone with the Wind or Putting off today what can be done tomorrow: Who hasn't thrilled to the last line of Margaret Mitchell's heroine, Scarlett O'Hara, when she resolves 'I'll think about that tomorrow!' as Rhett, the love of her life, leaves her. Procrastination is a great thief of time. It might seem like saving time to put something off, but usually the task is there to be done some time. As time passes the job may get more and more burdensome so that what might have taken five minutes builds up into a major task. If you are putting off something, think about what you are gaining by the delay. Are you avoiding something which you are afraid of? If so, how did you get into this situation? Is the fear logical? Are you putting this off because you never wanted to do it in the first place? Whatever the reason, make a decision to do this thing or not to do it and act on your decision.

Hansel and Gretel or Live now; pay later: It is true that Hansel and Gretel have a bad time. They are betrayed by their wicked mother and run away into the forest. But when they come upon the wonderful gingerbread house they get carried away by their craving, and think nothing of eating the house which could provide them with shelter. They ignore the warning 'Who is nibbling at my little house' and go on eating. In the end, of course, H & G end up happily ever after – such is the way of fairy tales. But if you are using your time in such a way that you are in danger of threatening your health or safety, maybe it's time to think again.

Sleeping Beauty or If you wait long enough, your prince will come. Well, of course Beauty's prince DID come – but can you guarantee that if you wait long enough without taking any initiatives your heart's desire will be achieved? We are only given one life and unlike the fairy tale do not get an extra 100 years to lie around waiting. Are you allowing some of your time to be stolen by leaving your ambitions unfulfilled? Why not start thinking about the practical possibilities of taking action to bring them about. You may not achieve all you want, but do you want to end your life full of regrets that you never tried?

> *Exercise: Imagine your life as a play, novel or fairy tale. What are the main themes? Is it a comedy, a drama, a tragedy? Who is the hero or heroine? Who is the villain? Are you in the first, second or third act? How does it look as if it's going to end? Who's in control of the script?*

Keeping a Time Diary

As an experiment and without referring to your diary, jot down everything you can remember doing in the past week. Try to account for every hour. You will probably find that, although you remember the main things you did, it will be difficult to remember in detail how the hours went. Our memory of how we spend time is very unreliable. This is why people needing to diet are usually asked to record what they eat each day, rather than just remember what they have eaten. The written record is more reliable in indicating which eating habits might need to be changed. In the same way, it is helpful to have a record of how you are actually spending time now, if you want to make some changes.

So before setting out to break the destructive circle identified in Chapter 1, take a little time to check where you are now in the journey of your life, so that any decisions you make about changing will move you in helpful, healthy directions.

> *Exercise: Imagine that time can take form and let the image take shape in your mind. Make a picture of how you see time. Your picture might take the form of a person, animal or shape. It might have a particular texture or colour. When you have completed the image, take time to explore its significance to you. For instance, do you see a friendly or hostile being? Is time always on your back chasing and harrying you? Has time for you become a barren, empty place? Is it like a will-o'-the-wisp – difficult to pin down and control?*

If you often feel as though the clock is always against you, it is time for you to turn time from your foe into your friend. Time can be on your side if you are willing to use it to your benefit. Taking control of your life means taking decisions. In the world of industry and commerce, managers are making decisions all the time with regard to the best use of their resources. Since making decisions is such an important element in time management, you need to be sure that you don't make any which cause you frustration, lower your self-esteem or increase your stress.

Take this opportunity to analyse how you use your time by keeping a time log – a record of your time investment.

One method of doing this is to keep a record of your activities over one week on a time chart as shown below. Begin with any day you like, but make sure you choose a typical week. If there is no particular pattern to your week, do the exercise for a month – or for whatever period is most appropriate. If the breakdown into two-hour slots doesn't suit you, create your own chart.

From the time you start, make sure you record eveything you do – even when you don't seem to be doing very much. If you spend half an hour on the phone trying to get through to someone, or if you have a twenty-minute rest, or take some time to skim the newspaper, make sure these times are included in your chart. They are the things we tend to forget – but each steals some time.

You can categorize the activities that suit your particular daily routine. For example at home you might include telephone calls, meeting friends, watching television, recreation, shopping, housework, eating, washing, child care, sleeping, evening classes, gardening, exercise and so on. If you are at work, categories which are helpful are administration tasks, meetings, socialising, refreshment breaks, interruptions and productive work.

Modify or add any categories to suit yourself so that this exercise will help you to understand more about how you spend your time. Taking stock in this way can help you separate and examine the various categories of time and how you use them. You can then decide whether you want to spend more or less time on particular activities.

Another possibility is to make a 'satisfaction' rating so that you can show in each segment of time how satisfied or unsatisfied you felt with that particular time. For instance if you are very happy with the way you spent that particular time you can mark it '+'; if you are not particularly happy but felt that what you did was necessary mark it '0'; if you are definitely unhappy about the way you used the time, use '−'. You could also add a brief comment about your thoughts and feelings at the time.

You can do the recording at the end of each day, although it is probably more effective if you do it throughout the day.

Time Chart:

	am						pm		
	6-8	8-10	10-12	12-2	2-4	4-6	6-8	8-10	10-12
Monday									
Tuesday									
Wednesday									
Thursday									
Friday									
Saturday									
Sunday									

At the end of the recording period, work out the percentage of time you spend in each category, for example: housework 20 per cent; child care 50 per cent; leisure 10 per cent and so on. This gives you a sense of just how your time is being used.

Keeping your Balance

This record will be of great help to you in deciding the changes which are necessary or possible for you to make. One important influence on how your time is spent is the need to play various roles and how you balance them. The chart below will give you a way of seeing your life in these terms. Fill it in as a bar chart to show what percentage of time is spent in your different roles. A list is suggested, but you can create one to fit your own situation.

Life Role   *% of Time*

	10	20	30	40	50	60	70+
Employee							
Father/Mother							
Son/Daughter							
Spouse							
Intimate Partner							
Consumer							
Friend							
Student							
Hobbies							
Churchgoer							
Housekeeper							
Etc.							

When you finish these exercises, ask yourself, 'How much of the time am I choosing what I do with my time?' Choice does not mean living your life only to fulfil your own needs without regard to anyone else. In order to maintain a reasonable lifestyle most of us have to do some things which are not particularly interesting or pleasant. The point of these exercises is to help you be clear as to the choices you do have and are making. For instance, supposing you are unhappy with your job and, given a straight choice, would resign tomorrow. You could, of course, do that – but the decision will have implications. If you were relying on the money you earned to maintain your lifestyle, how will you earn it? What will happen to any dependants you have? and so on. Probably, you will decide that continuing with the job is better than not – at least until you have thoroughly investigated the situation. This is a choice you are making.

Inside Out

Another way of looking at how you are using your time and energy is the 'Inside/Outside' concept. This exercise allows you to think how you are managing yourself and your environment:

> *Jot down on a piece of paper four or five occasions when you feel you were managing time really well. And then the same for when you felt things were not doing so well. For each occasion can you remember how you felt in yourself? Did you feel in or out of control? Were your feelings helping or hindering you in achieving what you wanted?*

You may find that there is a link between feeling you are using time well and feeling in control of yourself. Losing control of yourself contributes greatly to losing control of the situation.
This is another way of saying that what is outside us is a reflection of what is inside – and what is inside reflects the outside. Managing your inner self is an important element in managing the world outside.

Exercise: Draw a small circle to represent YOU; then draw a circle around that to represent those people who are closest to you – your family, partner, lover and so on; then draw a third circle around that to represent those who are less close, maybe your social friends; then draw a further outer circle to represent the next level, perhaps work colleagues. Continue drawing circles and label each level until you have drawn your world in this way. The last circle might be labelled for the community/society you live in.

Your diagram probably looks a bit like a shooting target with you at the centre. Give yourself some time to consider how your world looks to you. Write down what seems to be going well in each of the circles. How are you using your time, your talents, your skills, your knowledge with the people in each circle? The next stage would be to consider what is not going well in each circle. How are you contributing to the problems? Is there some way in which you are not using your resources as well as possible? Are you aware of any unresolved pressures, problems or issues?

This exercise is about YOU as the centre of your world and encourages you to identify how you are contributing to what is going right and what is going wrong.

The intention of this collection of exercises is to give you ideas about how to analyse what is happening to your time at the moment. Every person is unique so there is no *right* way to do this analysis. If the structures I have suggested don't suit you, make up other ones for yourself.

A Pyramid of Needs

If you are feeling very unsatisfied and unhappy with how your life is going at the moment, another angle of analysis is to consider how your needs are being met.

An American psychologist, Abraham Maslow, viewed human needs in a hierarchical way. He described how our needs can be arranged in an order, some of which have to be satisfied before we can or want to address ourselves to a higher level of need. He worked out the pyramid of psychological needs in this way.

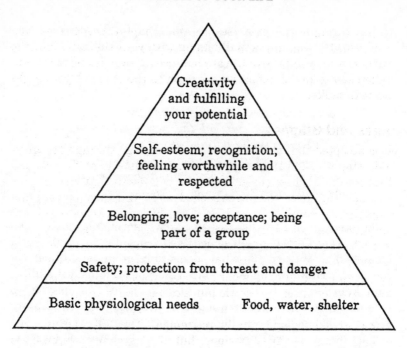

The diagram shows the order in which he believed we experience our needs. Those needs at the bottom of the pyramid have to be met before we can move up to the next level. So if, for instance, your main concern is getting an income just to keep yourself alive you are not likely to be using up much time contemplating the infinite meaning of the universe! However we have needs right up the pyramid and if some categories are not being met at all, life is bound to feel somewhat empty and pointless.

> *Exercise: Using the information from your time log, sort your main activities into the levels of the pyramid. Questions you could ask yourself about the result include, 'What does this say about how I am meeting my needs? Am I stuck on one level? Are there important needs not being met at all? Am I trying to meet needs on higher levels, without paying attention to the lower level needs? Do I want to change anything as a result of this?*

Going through the exercises in this chapter has helped you analyse what you are actually doing with your time and how the various roles you play in life are balanced. There is one more consideration to make before we move on to the changes you might want to make.

Ages and Stages

It is accepted that children and adolescents go through recognizable stages of development, but what is sometimes forgotten is that adults also go through phases of growth and change. It's assumed that once you have reached adulthood, development and change have come to an end. So if you haven't reached a point of stability you can easily feel you have failed in some way.

Each stage of life brings its own particular tasks. Adolescents, for example, need to gain independence from their parents and find their own identity; in our early twenties we have to establish a lifestyle for ourselves, settle into a career and develop long-term relationships; we may then move into stages of parenthood, grandparenthood and, finally, retirement. The difference in focus of each stage is fairly obvious, but the psychological changes which each requires may not be so clear.

There is a powerful mythology surrounding the expectations of different age groups. For example, young adults are supposed to be full of energy, seeking independence and full of ambition. If you happen to be a tired, depressed twenty-five year old who is finding it hard to get a job, you have reason to be doubly depressed! Not only is your life unsatisfactory at the moment, but you are not supposed to feel like this. In middle age you are supposed to be satisfied, fulfilled and steadily living your life; so how can you make sense of feeling restless, moody or unhappy. The over sixties are assumed to be slowing down and stay-at-home; at this age you are supposed to lose your physical attractiveness and usefulness. What if you are a fit, sixty-five year old who has just fallen in love with someone new?

The Expectations of Others

There are strong cultural expectations as to appropriate behaviour in adulthood. For instance each culture has definite ideas as to when people should marry, when they should finish their education, when they should become independent and so on. Anyone who seems to deviate from the expected can feel very much 'out of step' which adds to the level of stress they are already experiencing. The expectations which we inherit from our culture may also be out-of-date. For instance, I am writing this in a time of recession where more and more people are finding it hard to get or keep a job and set up or maintain a home for themselves. Naturally, the feelings of anger, frustration, anxiety and so on which arise as a result of this situation add to the stress caused by failing to reach the powerful expectations of a society which has a strong value system based on independence and the work ethic.

Rather than trying to work out whether you are 'in step' with the expectations surrounding your particular age, let's explore the features of different life stages. This will help you determine which tasks are appropriate to the stage of development you are now facing and what obstacles you might need to overcome. The suggested age range for each stage is a combination of work by several writers and researchers, including Gail Sheehy in her books *Passages* and *Pathfinders*. But, these are offered only as a guideline. If you find that you are ahead or behind, this is a chance to re-evaluate where you are and what you are doing at this point. Maybe you are facing tasks which are inappropriate for your particular stage. Maybe you are experiencing the characteristic feelings caused by questioning your life's past goals and beliefs which so often mark the passage from one stage to another.

Ages and Stages of Adult Development

Establishing Adulthood between ages twenty and twenty-eight
This is a time when we are, perhaps for the first time, 'on our own', exploring commitments to work, long-term loving relationships, marriage. It is not so much a time of deep analysis – rather time to get on with being independent in the world. The kind of questions which surface are 'What is the right career for me?' 'How can I find the right person for me?' Whereas in adolescence the most important thing seems to be independence, at this stage the idea of commitment seems more valuable. Life feels more like something to be defined and controlled rather than an open book

in which anything can happen. The future lies ahead, full of possibilities.

Making Adjustments (between ages twenty-eight and thirty-two)
Around the age of thirty, the lifestyle we have created may need adjustment. Life can seem much more complex than it appeared. Relationships or career plans that were intended to be long-term come in for reassessment. Maybe the future which seemed so full of possibilities has turned out to be much more restricted than you expected, and the optimism of early adulthood feels as though it was unrealistic.

This is a time of change for many people as they consider the implications of continuing with their choices. Questions like 'What do I really want out of life?' 'How can I find out about myself?' are relevant at this time. Preoccupations include making enough money to live the way you want. The search for self-identity becomes important and life can seem uncertain and full of crucial decisions. If you have not already started a family, whether or not to have children is a question which is often raised at this time. For women in our society this is a crucial decision if they have a career for it may feel as if they have to choose between motherhood and their job.

Settling Down (between ages thirty-two and thirty-nine) After the confusions of the previous stage of adjustment, we tend to get on with whatever lifestyle we have developed. Some people experience discomfort around the age of thirty-five, as if they have the first awareness that life will not last forever. After all, this is half-way to 'three-score years and ten' so it is an important marker. It's also a time when people seem to seek a guide or mentor to help with the problems which seem to rear their heads at this stage. If you have a career this will be a time of wanting to achieve some recognition of success. Life might not seem so exciting and you may feel the need for more support. For the first time the future seems limited by time.

Midlife Shift (between ages thirty-nine and forty-five) Anyone who watches television drama, goes to the cinema or reads novels will be very familiar with the phenomenon of the 'midlife crisis'. For many people it is a period of acute personal discomfort. We become more aware of the limits which exist to fulfilling our goals. We are brought face-to-face with the reality of our achievements as compared to our youthful dreams.

For some, this transition is just a marker, for others a painful time of crisis. People often talk of feeling lonely – even though they may be a member of a family and have many friends, they realize they are alone on this particular journey. Children are growing up and away and, on the other hand, ageing parents are looking for support. Questions such as 'What's happened to my life?' 'What have I really achieved?' 'When am I going to have what I want?' 'Why can't they accept me for what I am, not what they expect me to be?' 'Is this going to be my last chance to succeed?' arise at this time.

Some people completely change their direction at this time, turning to a new career or a new relationship.

Re-balancing and Renewal (between ages forty-five and sixty) For those people who successfully negotiate their midlife transition this can feel like the best stage of all. In a career, status and recognition often come at this stage, perhaps with important promotion. On the other hand, for some people it is a time when they feel hopeless about gaining recognition. The financial responsibilities of parenthood diminish as children leave home. Money, in any case, often seems less important as people find they become more introspective, listening more to their inner voice than to external demands. People become clearer and more confident about their values. The rush which we may experience in our earlier years seems to slow down and we have more time to be and value ourselves. Women experience a physical reminder of the passing of time as they move through the menopause, a time which can sometimes be both physically uncomfortable and psychologically troubled.

Arriving at Maturity (sixty plus) At this stage, we can accept ourselves and come to grips with what we have and haven't achieved. It can be a time of starting something we have always wanted to do because this might be the last opportunity. For those with a career, retirement is on the horizon and this can be stressful for a person whose life has been very focused on work. And this is, of course, a time of ageing. Partners and friends may die or become ill. Our own health may deteriorate. Our mortality, which may up to now have seemed unreal, may suddenly become very real indeed.

> *Exercise: Before continuing to read on, take a moment to reflect on the life stage you have reached.*
>
> - *What do you see as the main life tasks which face you now?*
> - *What life stages are the people you live with facing?*
> - *Is there anything unfinished from previous life styles?*
> - *Is there anything that needs to change in order that you achieve what you want at this time in your life?*

Making Use of Your Time Analysis

Now is the time to return to the analysis of your use of time.

> *Exercise: (Part 1) At the end of Chapter 1, you made a picture of how your time looked. Have another look at it and on a fresh piece of paper, draw the picture of how you would like to be if you had absolutely free choice. This is a fantasy exercise, so you can give full rein to your imagination! It doesn't matter too much at this stage whether what you want is realistic. When you have finished, take some time to look at what you have produced. Be aware of how you think and feel about it.*
>
> *Now for Part 2. Taking both your pictures into account, make a third which incorporates those things you know you have to do, even though given free choice you wouldn't, as well as at least some of those things which you want to do, but don't have time for at the moment. This picture will probably be more realistic than the second, but closer to how you want your life to be than the first.*

This exercise leads on to the analysis of your time diary. To start off, make a list of all the activities (or categories of activities) that make up your use of time at the moment. You might have a list which looks like:

> Work
> Reading
> Shopping
> Child Care
> Leisure
> Sport
> Time for thinking
> Hobbies

The list should suit your particular circumstances. For instance, if you want to use these exercises to organize the time you spend at work better, the category 'work' would have to be broken down into the various components:

> Dealing with correspondence
> Attending meetings
> Answering telephone
> Writing reports
> Travelling
>   and so on.

Try to keep the list no longer than ten headings, otherwise the exercise can get too complicated. When you are satisfied with your list, work out roughly how much time you ought or want to be spending on each of the activities, bearing in mind the kind of life you want to be living. It's useful to refer to your third drawing from the last exercise. For instance, if you are a parent wanting more time to spend on your own pursuits, when you come to look closely at your time diary to see where time could be saved, you probably won't want to consider cutting down the time you spend with the children, but you might look to other categories to see if time can be saved.

> *Exercise: These next four exercises will help you to make these kind of decisions:*

STAGE 1: Going through your time log, list every activity which appears.

STAGE 2: Now list these in order of importance as you see them in relation to how you want to be spending your time.

STAGE 3: To identify the areas where you could make changes, mark each time with the actual number of hours each day you spend on them (A); how much time you think you ought to want to spend on them (B); and the time difference if there is one (C)

STAGE 4: List the items from the last stage which have time differences. These are the areas in which you can begin to effect changes.

As a result of this exercise you may be able to identify several ways in which you can begin changing. There might be some very simple ways of saving time which you can begin right away. Others may not be so simple and you may have to discuss them with anyone who might be affected by your decisions. You need therefore to look at the things you want to change and decide:

- which things you can change alone
- which you would have to discuss with others
- which can't be changed now but might be in the future
- which things are not within your power to change at all

At this point give yourself a treat! If you have been doing all the exercises in this chapter, you will have been working hard and deserve a reward. Take a break before considering your next move.

3

TIME FOR STROKES

Imagine that you are walking down a corridor. Someone you know is coming from the other direction. You smile as you pass each other and say 'Hello'; the other person answers 'Hi! How are you?' You have acknowledged each other or, in other words, you have exchanged *strokes*. This chapter is about the importance of strokes and how we structure time in order to maintain our supply.

In the previous chapter we looked at Abraham Maslow's idea that our physical and psychological needs can be seen as a pyramid, with the most basic needs at the base. He makes the point that in order for us to survive and develop happy and healthy lives, our basic physical needs for air, water, food, shelter and so on have to be met. We need to feel safe and secure.

Our Psychological Needs

Another psychologist, Eric Berne who was the originator of a theory about human development called Transactional Analysis, added to this idea. He identified stimulation, structure and recognition as among the needs which we seek to meet. He called them *hungers*, to emphasize the strength with which we experience them. If we are deprived of any of our physical basic needs, the search for them will take over. Remember the last time you felt very hungry or thirsty and how that took over whatever else you were thinking or doing until you could eat and drink. Our psychological needs affect us in much the same way, but the search for them is largely unconscious. Thus we sometimes engage in behaviour to meet our needs without really being aware of what we are doing.

> *Exercise: Recall a recent time when you felt surprised or confused about the way you were behaving. Perhaps you suddenly got angry and shouted at someone; dropped and broke something; told a joke; lit a cigarette and so on. Can you work out what need was being fulfilled for you by this behaviour?*

Eric Berne was interested in the work of researchers in human and animal development, and in particular was influenced by a well-known investigation by Rene Spitz who had observed babies brought up in a children's home. They were well fed, kept clean and warm. Yet they were more likely to experience physical and emotional difficulties than were children brought up by their mothers or other direct carers. Spitz concluded that what the children in the home lacked was stimulation. Not only did they have little to look at all day except the white walls of their rooms, but they had little physical contact with those who looked after them. They lacked the touching, cuddling and stroking which babies would normally get from the people taking care of them.

Contact and Communication

Eric Berne proposed that when we become adults we don't lose this need for physical contact, even though we live in a society which to a large extent doesn't allow a great deal of touching. Think about the last few days and add up the amount of time you have spent touching or being touched by someone. If you are living an ordinary sort of life, I expect there have been large periods of time when you have not been in such close contact with another person.

So what happens to this need for contact? Berne's idea was that we learned to substitute other forms of recognition in its place. A smile, a compliment or even a frown or insult all show us that our existence has been recognized. He coined the word 'stroke' to describe a communication with someone else which causes us to feel something.

In order to survive and to feel satisfied with our lives, we develop ways of getting our needs met. How we go about this depends a great deal on our early experiences of getting and giving strokes. Because physical stroking is an important component in our survival as an infant, the quality of the strokes we received helped us define our world as rough, gentle, secure, indifferent, loving, hostile and so on.

Strokes are powerful motivators. Children are encouraged to modify their natural behaviour and learn social behaviour as a result of the reward or deprivation of strokes by parents and carers. As infants we test out all sorts of behaviours in order to find out which ones will give us the strokes we need. When something we do turns out to earn strokes, we are likely to repeat it. Each time it gets a further stroke, we become ever more ready to use that behaviour in future and so a pattern develops. As a general rule, we work on the principle that 'any stroke is better than no stroke.' If there aren't enough positive strokes to meet our needs, we will go ahead to seek negative strokes or 'slaps'.

We have all learned individual ways to give and get strokes in the families where we were raised. We get into the habit of expecting strokes or slaps for particular behaviour and tend to go on expecting them, unless we make a conscious decision to change. You can test out this idea for yourself with this exercise.

> *Exercise: This exercise is intended to help you connect your early experiences of getting attention with the present day. There are many things you could get attention for as a child. Start by thinking about the kind of things you remember getting attention for when you were young. It might have come in the positive form of praise, smiles, etc. or the negative form of rebukes, frowns, etc. Use the following list as a guide, adding items of your own. Mark any of the items which are true for you with a tick for positive or a cross if it was negative.*

When I was young I got strokes for:

- just being me; I didn't have to do anything in particular;
- getting good marks at school;

- passing exams; getting top marks;
- being good at sport;
- being willing to have a go at anything;
- being persistent;
- being independent;
- making people laugh;
- getting things done quickly;
- not making a fuss;
- helping others;
- putting others first;
- trying difficult things;
- joining clubs or teams;
- taking a leadership role;
- keeping busy;
- being stupid or clumsy;
- being quiet and unobtrusive;
- being loud and demanding;
- not standing out or being different;
- doing my best even when I didn't succeed;
- being untidy or dirty;
- saying 'Yes' when asked to do something;
- saying 'No' when asked to do something;
- asking 'Why?';
- taking new opportunities;
- taking risks;
- doing things without being asked;
- being ill.

Add any which are true for you but not on the list.

The pattern of ticks and crosses will show the kind of strokes or slaps you received early in your life. It may also enlighten you as to your present pattern. You could discuss this with someone who knows you well enough to tell you what they have noticed.

This exercise could help you notice whether:

- any of the things for which you got strokes in your childhood are still important;

- any of them are missing from your life;

- there are other kinds of strokes you would like to get;

- the way your life is organized at the moment conflicts with the possibility of getting the kind of recognition you want;

- there are strokes you are receiving for things you didn't mark in the exercise. If this is so it is possible that you don't hear or accept or value recognition that you are getting.

In our early childhood there were times when we experienced not getting the positive strokes we needed or wanted. We knew instinctively that we needed strokes and because of this any strokes were better than none. So when we felt deprived of positive strokes we worked out ways of getting negative ones because, although they may have been painful, they were better than nothing.

Imagine a scene in the kitchen; mother is at the sink peeling potatoes for the evening meal and listening to the radio; Tom aged four is in another room watching TV; programme ends; Tom gets bored and wanders into the kitchen. All he can see is mother's back; she is engrossed in the radio and hurrying to get the meal ready. She has no attention spare for Tom. He potters around for a bit, but still no attention; he accidentally knocks over a dish which breaks all over the floor – then he gets attention! Mother turns, shouts, tells Tom in no uncertain terms what a nuisance he is! None of this is pleasant for Tom – but it's better than being ignored. Maybe if this kind of thing has happened before he has realized that knocking things over will work as a stroke-getter!

The Price of Strokes

Exercise: How did you get strokes in your family when you were a child? Did you have to compete with other siblings? Were your parents or carers generous or mean when it came to giving strokes?

Did strokes have a price such as keeping clean or being good?

That exercise introduces the idea of strokes at a price. You get some strokes because of who and what you are. That means they are free and unconditional; they don't depend on you having to do anything. Examples are 'I love you'; 'It's lovely having you around'. Unconditional negative strokes would be 'I hate you', 'I don't like red-headed people – it's your red hair that's the problem!' Other strokes, however, are given on condition that you behave in a certain way. Conditional strokes can be costly. 'That was a marvellous meal you cooked,' 'I really appreciate you when you don't interrupt me,' are examples of positive conditional strokes. 'I hate your socks!' 'I'll be very cross if you don't keep clean,' are both negative and conditional.

Some strokes sound as if they are free but actually have a hidden cost. For instance 'I can see that you are doing well – up to a point,' 'You're looking great – it's a pity the shoes don't match your coat.' These could be called counterfeit strokes. It sounds as if you are getting something really worthwhile but it ends up spoilt or less valuable than you expected. Sometimes these counterfeit strokes have a sting in the tail that turns them into a slap.

Then there are the kind of strokes that are devalued because they go too far; 'How wonderful to see you! You really are the most marvellous person. I am just so pleased that you came – everyone loves you so much. That last book you wrote was fantastically inspiring . . .' and so on. These have been described as marshmallow or plastic – apparently sweet and valuable but actually insubstantial and not the real thing. On the other hand, some people have trouble in giving any positive strokes at all. Maybe they come from a family where positive stroking was scarce. Cultural backgrounds also play a part. We can feel uncomfortable in the company of someone who has a very different stroke pattern from our own. For instance, a person from, say, a Caribbean or Latin culture, where strokes are liberally distributed, may experience someone from Scandinavia or Britain as cold and reserved because their strokes are more sparingly given.

Exercise: Draw a stroke bar chart like the one below to show the amount of each kind of stroke you receive.

	Positive Unconditional 'I love you'	Negative Unconditional 'I hate you'	Positive Conditional 'You've done a good job'	Negative Conditional 'You've done a poor job'
6				
5				
4				
3				
2				
1				

Now draw a similar chart showing strokes that you give. Redraw the graphs showing any changes that you would like made.

Identify your own favourite strokes and then ask other people who are important in your life what their favourite strokes are. You may be surprised at the differences in people's preferences. We tend to give the strokes that we would like to get. Are there any strokes you are giving because you are not getting them?

Claude Steiner, who developed this idea of a stroke economy, describes how parents use strokes as a way of controlling their children's behaviour and that as a result children may come to believe that:

• You shouldn't give strokes freely or there won't be enough to go around. Every time you give a stroke to someone you have reduced your own supply.

- You shouldn't ask for strokes when you need them. If you do they will lose their value and you will be seen as demanding.

- You shouldn't show that you want strokes. The polite thing to do with strokes that you really want given is to return the stroke or deny that you wanted it otherwise you would be seen as weak or unable to cope.

- You shouldn't reject strokes when you don't want them. If you want to be liked by people you have to accept whatever they give you.

- You shouldn't give yourself strokes. Looking after yourself in this way could be seen as talking big and boasting.

> *Exercise: Looking back at the stroke graph you have just drawn, is there any evidence that you might be operating unconsciously from any of the above 'rules'. If so, can you see how you might be depriving yourself of potential good feelings.*

Are you restricting your supply of strokes because of the early childhood decisions you made in response to your perceptions of pressure from parents? Now, as a grown-up you are in a position to reassess these decisions and change them if you want.

One very common myth is that 'strokes you have to ask for are worthless'. Actually they are likely to be as valuable as any others. Suppose you are feeling very low and would like a comforting cuddle from a friend you happen to be with. If you ask for it and get it, it is just as good a cuddle as the one you might get by waiting and hoping. You could be thinking, 'But if I ask, the other person will only give me what I want just to be polite.' This might be true or it might not. You always have the chance to check it out with them. It's possible that the other person has been longing to comfort you but was afraid of embarrassing you or of being rejected.

> *Exercise: Discuss with your family and friends 'What are your favourite kinds of strokes?' Some people like talking strokes, others prefer physical*

cuddling strokes. Some want undivided attention;
others favour the strokes that come from doing
activities together.

We are each a powerful source of strokes for ourselves, but many
of us were taught by our parents and teachers that it was 'showing off' or boastful to be proud or pleased with ourselves. Someone
who did nothing else but praise themselves would be pretty un-
bearable but some of us go to the other extreme. We learned those
childhood lessons so well we belittle our achievements even to
ourselves.

> *Exercise: Write on a large sheet of paper all your*
> *achievements – large and small. Remember that*
> *learning to walk and talk were great achievements*
> *at the time! If you have the space, pin the paper up*
> *where you can see it often or keep it where it is*
> *easily to hand. Keep adding to it every time you*
> *think of something you may have left out.*
>   *Another suggestion is to make a list of ten ways*
> *you could give yourself a positive stroke. For in-*
> *stance, taking a hot, scented bath; listening to a*
> *favourite piece of music; sitting in the sun; buying*
> *a new hat; reading an enjoyable book; going for a*
> *walk; phoning up a friend. Check that they really*
> *are positive and unconditional. It is important, for*
> *instance, that you don't think of these things as 're-*
> *wards' for being good, but that you give them to*
> *yourself for your own sake.*

Structuring Time

Recognizing the importance of strokes leads on to time management. If, in order to survive, we must get our basic needs met then
we need to structure our time in order to do this. An intricate
social structure has evolved to enable us to meet our physical and
psychological needs. If they are not met we are in serious trouble
as far as our continued survival is concerned. Strokes are basic to
our psychological survival; another of Eric Berne's ideas was to
describe how we structured our time in order to search for them.

He suggests six different ways of spending time, each one being a potential source of strokes and each having its advantages and disadvantages.

Withdrawal: Sometimes, when we don't find enough satisfaction in the way we are living, we tend to go inside ourselves to find strokes. You might, for instance, withdraw physically by going to another room, reading a book or going to sleep. Or you might withdraw mentally, so that although you are still with other people, your mind is elsewhere. Daydreaming allows us to make up fantasies about our world – we can see ourselves achieving great accomplishments, having wonderful love affairs or making a lot of money. Television and cinema are ways of getting strokes while we are alone – by identifying with the leading character we can vicariously experience his or her feelings.

At its most positive, Withdrawal leads to the peace and enlightenment of meditation or prayer, providing a haven of freedom, independence and privacy. If your stroke economy is healthy and you have a good supply, retreating from the pressures of life by withdrawing from time to time can be extremely therapeutic. You can disengage momentarily by daydreaming; you can give yourself time to go for a walk, read a magazine, absorb yourself in a hobby. You can withdraw for longer periods going away to a hotel or a retreat house. These breaks give you time to refuel your energy, to make plans and decisions so that when you return you are better able to face life.

However, when you are withdrawn you are relying on your internal supply of strokes and so spending too much time in this way runs the risk of you becoming deprived. Simply, you are spending your currency without replacing it. At its most negative, Withdrawal can lead to feelings of isolation and loneliness. Our contact with others enables us, for instance, to distinguish between our fantasies and reality. A lack of contact makes it harder to ensure that our perceptions of our world are accurate.

> *Exercise: Thinking back over the past week, have there been any times when you have mentally or physically withdrawn from what has been happening? What was going on for you at the time?*

Were you left with positive feelings such as being
rested, restimulated, regenerated or negative feel-
ings like depression, sadness, loneliness?

Ritual: A Ritual is a commonly agreed way of acting; a safe predictable way of getting strokes. Rituals range from simple social
exchanges, a quick exchange of 'Hellos' or 'Good Evenings' to
elaborate ceremonial like church services or the Opening of Par-
liament. A typical Ritual conversation might go something like
this:

Elaine: Hello, John. How are you?

John: Hi, Elaine. Nice to see you. I'm fine. How are you?

Elaine: I'm well, thanks. How are the kids?

John: Kids are well, thanks. How are yours?

Elaine: Both doing fine, thanks. Are you busy these days?

John: Yes, very. You, too?

Elaine: Yes. It's great to see you again.

John: Same here. Give my regards to Alan.

Elaine: Sure. Mine to Joyce. See you soon, I hope.

Both Elaine and John are giving each other strokes of attention,
but the contact is not very deep. It sounds like a script which they
have spoken many times before, and probably they will have forgotten the contact five minutes after they leave each other.

We all learned the Rituals which were part of our family culture. If you are British, you will probably have learned that if
someone says 'How do you do?' you are supposed to answer with
the same question; if you are American when you meet someone
you probably start with 'Hi!'; if you are French, you are likely to
greet someone by kissing them on both cheeks; and so on.

Rituals are useful because they provide structures for potentially difficult or risky situations: meeting new people, for instance or structuring a meeting. Think what it would be like if, when you met someone new and said 'Hello!', they didn't respond to you. Life without these social rituals would feel strange and often uncomfortable.

However, on the negative side, if your time is structured primarily in Ritual you probably feel that your life is somewhat empty. Other people are likely to experience you as polite and pleasant, but you might also come over as rather shallow because Rituals tend to cover up our inner thoughts and feelings.

> *Exercise: Take a typical day in your life and list any Rituals you engaged in. What purpose did they fulfil for you? How did they help you? Is there any way in which they prevented you making contact?*

Pastimes: We can spend time with other people pleasantly passing the time by sharing our opinions, thoughts or feelings about relatively safe topics. These conversations are rather like Rituals in that things proceed in a familiar way, although it is not programmed so strictly. While engaging in a Pastime, the participants talk *about* something but *do* nothing.

Pastimes are often predictable – the same people say the same things and you almost know in advance what will be said. Pastimes include, for instance, talking about what's wrong with the world, children, work, the education system, cars, football, clothes, holidays and so on. Someone might say, 'Did you see the TV play on Thursday night?' Then there will be an exchange of views on the play and someone might go on 'There was an even better one on Friday, did anyone see that?' and so the conversation will continue.

Gossip is a Pastime, 'Have you heard the latest about Tony and Ellen.' Sometimes they are about what's wrong with things. 'Children never ...' 'Bosses always ...' 'Politicians ought to ...'. It doesn't really matter whether the person you are with agrees or disagrees with you. Either way you get a lot of contact. Although if you were only to spend your time in this way you would probably get bored after a while. Pastimes are a good way of making contact with people but rarely lead to anything more than superficial communication.

> *Exercise: What are your favourite Pastimes? How much of your time this week has been spent this way?*

Activity: The fourth way in which we can spend our time is by doing tasks or Activities; this is when our energy is directed to something outside ourselves. Work, hobbies and chores are common examples and many of us spend a great deal of our time involved in this way. Activities can provide valuable strokes both from the people involved in sharing the task and from yourself when you are satisfied with a job well done. On the other hand, negative strokes might be the result when the task is not completed or when you maybe have to face your own inability.

Strokes for Activities can come from direct awards like examination marks, cups and trophies and, of course, salary cheques. There are advantages and disadvantages with these strokes too. The advantage of using activity to structure time is that, as well as the direct strokes, activities provide a relatively safe structure within which to receive and give personal strokes. On the negative side, a person who uses this as a main method can easily become a workaholic. Workaholics are generally so tied up with activities that they have no chance to share closeness or fun with others. They also run the risk of not giving themselves the time to be in touch with themselves.

> *Exercise: Make a list of the Activities which you have carried out in the past week or so. What strokes did they produce for you? What strokes have you given yourself as a result of what you accomplished?*

Games: Have you ever found yourself in a situation which feels familiar but ends up with you and anyone else involved feeling bad. Afterwards you might have said to yourself something like: 'Why does this keep on happening to me?'; 'How on earth did that happen?' You might have felt surprised at the way things turned out but at the same time realized that this kind of thing seems to keep on happening.

If this has happened to you, then you were probably engaged in a psychological Game. Games are a way of structuring time when you are trying to fulfil a need and don't know any other way to do it. Unlike ordinary games like tennis or dominoes, we don't know when we are playing them. However they are similar to ordinary games in that they are played to a set of predictable rules. Here are a couple of examples:

Sarah works in a café and is talking to a customer who is looking very down and depressed.

Customer: I'm having a terrible time. I've been made redundant and my wife's left me. I can't pay the mortgage and I just don't know what to do.

Sarah: Oh how awful! I'm so sorry. Is there anything I can do to help?

Customer: I don't know. I don't know what anyone can do.

Sarah: I know. Here's the local paper. Why don't you look through it to see if there's a job available?

Customer: I've been doing that. I've written off for hundreds of jobs but never get any interviews.

Sarah: Oh, that's a shame. Well, why don't you go to the mortgage company and explain. They'll probably make some arrangement to help you.

Customer: Yes, but I don't think they'd be willing to let me off payments for long.

Sarah:	Why don't you try to make it up with your wife? You'd be happier then.
Customer:	Oh, no! I couldn't do that – anyway she wouldn't listen to me.
Sarah:	[. . . silence. She racks her brains to come up with something to help but can't think of anything.]
Customer:	[. . . sighs and starts to leave.] There's no point in talking about it. No-one can ever help me because no-one really cares.

Sarah feels depressed. She's tried her best to help and can't understand why the customer won't pull himself together. Meantime, the customer is walking down the street feeling cross that Sarah couldn't come up with anything and convinced that no-one will ever be able to help.

This is a popular Game called 'Why Don't You? Yes, But'. For both Sarah and the customer it is a replay of similar past scenes.

When people play a Game they are communicating on more than one level. Every Game has a hidden agenda. People playing Games are not really talking about what it sounds as if they're talking about. They are out to prove that an early decision they made about the nature of the world is true.

'Ain't It Awful' shows how a Game can prevent problem solving. I remember an occasion when I was due to teach a group of advice workers. That morning the funding arrangements for that year were announced and this particular group had been awarded extra funds for opening another centre. On my way to the training session I wondered what kind of celebration we might have. When I arrived the atmosphere was excited and expectant. Then Shirley, one of the managers, arrived. She came into the room looking downcast and worried. Throwing herself into the nearest chair she looked around the group and complained, 'It's going to be difficult to decide where to site this new centre and I don't know how we're going to get people to staff it.'

Shirley was very dedicated and a hard worker. Everyone felt that she was doing a wonderful job in helping to run the centres and she appeared, on the surface, to be very successful. Early experiences led her to believe that nothing would ever go right for her. This didn't stop her from trying; in fact one of the reasons that she was so successful is that she worked so hard. However, her internal belief sabotaged her energy even when there was the potential for success. The effect on her was that she was left feeling depressed. The effect on the others in the group was that they were tempted to feel guilty at their high spirits.

'See What You Made Me Do' is a common blaming Game. A person makes a mistake in the presence of someone else and then blames that mistake on the other person. For example, Jack is concentrating on his homework. His brother approaches and looks over Jack's shoulder. Jack makes a mistake. Rather than take responsibility for his error, Jack rounds angrily on his brother, 'See what you made me do!' Jack is left feeling angry about his brother and righteous about himself. This righteous feeling of 'Nothing is ever my fault – it's always someone else's' will lead to feelings of powerlessness. It might lead to Jack's isolation because after enough experiences of being blamed, people tend to avoid the blamer.

Eric Berne identified many common themes of the Games people play and his book *Games People Play* (Penguin 1968) describes these and others.

Another facet of 'Game-playing' is that the players seem to take on one of three roles, which are swapped as the Game continues.

Stephen Karpman, another of the developers of Transactional Analysis devised a deceptively simple idea for analysing these Game roles which he called 'The Drama Triangle'. The three roles in the drama are Persecutor, Victim and Rescuer. A Persecutor is someone who puts other people down, by belittling or punishing them. A Rescuer, on the other hand, is very helpful, but does things for which people haven't actually asked. It is as if they offer help because of their belief that the other person is not capable of helping themselves. A Victim feels helpless, discounting his or her abilities and seeming to invite others to do the same. As the Game progresses the roles change, so for instance a Persecutor may feel guilty, try to rescue their partner only to find the Victim has turned Persecutor so that they now find themselves the Victim.

Which Games do you Play?

Take another look at the *'Why Don't You, Yes But . . .'* Game between Sarah and the customer. The customer starts off in the Victim position and Sarah takes up the Rescuer role. When the customer gets up to leave he turns into Persecutor – criticising 'people' for not helping him. Sarah feels like a victim – she's tried her best but the customer is unwilling to help himself and not at all grateful for her efforts.

> *Exercise: Take one minute to write down all the words you can think of that might describe a Persecutor. Do the same for a Rescuer and for a Victim.*
>
> *Can you think of any people you know who seem to play out these roles in their life?*
>
> *Can you think of any times when you slip into one or other of the roles? What is the usual outcome?*

We all play Games from time to time. When you are identifying your own time-structuring patterns in the following exercises, label as 'Games' the time you spend in the kind of interchange I have just described. It's repetitive for you. It ends up with you feeling bad. And at some point, it entails a moment when you ask yourself 'What just happened?' and you get a feeling of confusion. One way of looking at Games is that they are replays of childhood strategies that are no longer appropriate to us as grown-ups.

They are a predictable source of strokes – although the strokes will turn out to be negative in the end. A relationship in which the communication was entirely through Games would feel unsatisfactory and hollow because it wouldn't feel very spontaneous and the communication would avoid deeper feelings.

According to Eric Berne there are six advantages of Game-playing:

1 *They help to confirm our internal beliefs:* In an earlier chapter

I suggested that when we were children we each created a set of beliefs about the nature of the world and our place in it. Because Games are so predictable, in playing them we can continue to prove that what we believe is actually right. For instance each time Sarah plays 'Why Don't You . . .' she ends up with the familiar feeling that she is responsible for someone else's happiness, and that she will never be able to do enough.

2 *If we play Games, we don't have to challenge our internal beliefs:* When Jack plays 'See What You Made Me Do', he doesn't have to feel the anxiety of facing up to taking responsibility for his mistake.

3 *When we are in the midst of a Game it feels like we are in intimate contact with someone:* The Game 'Why Don't You, Yes But . . .' can, for instance, include a long discussion about different options for action. This feels to the people involved as if they are being open and spontaneous with each other even though each is repeating an old pattern.

4 *They help with our social life:* Finding someone to play 'Ain't It Awful' with you, means you are guaranteed hours of contact and conversation. If you're at a party or in a bar, lots of people can join in and the time passes pleasantly enough in a social situation.

5 *We get more strokes:* Admittedly, Games usually end with negative strokes – but you will remember that slaps are better than no strokes at all. Take, for example, the customer in the first example. Perhaps, as a child he found positive strokes were hard to come by, and so found more predictable ways of getting negative strokes. Each time he refuses to consider an option, he increases his feeling that no-one will be able to help.

6 *They confirm our general view of life:* From our earliest days we experience ourselves as being acceptable or not. Simply, we can think of ourselves and other people as OK or Not OK. The games we play will confirm whichever position we take. For instance, 'Why Don't You, Yes But' leaves Sarah feeling that she's OK but that the customer is not. ('You just can't help some people!'). The customer, of course, leaves feeling he is not OK and neither is anyone else. ('No-one can help me!)

Exercise: Think about something that keeps on happening to you, and leaves you with a familiar negative feeling. Give this scenario a name which describes the theme. What is it that you are not saying to the other person involved? Which of the six advantages listed above are you getting?

Intimacy: Finally, there's intimacy. Intimacy is often thought to be the most risky and the most rewarding of all ways of structuring time. It is based on the idea that 'I'm acceptable to me and you're acceptable to me' and involves sharing feelings, thoughts and experiences openly and honestly. When we are in intimate contact we give each other unconditional strokes without feeling defensive. There are no 'secret messages' as in games. Although the effects of such strokes are particularly pleasant and gratifying, the demands of total honesty would be too difficult for us to manage most of the time. When we are absolutely open about our thoughts and feelings, we feel vulnerable. It is as if we have no defence against being hurt or exploited. This is why we often choose ways of structuring time that feel safer because our innermost self is defended.

Intimacy might arise from a brief contact or from a lifetime relationship. These are some examples:

- two friends meeting each other after a long time, laughing and hugging and exchanging news;

- one mother seeing another struggling to contain a boisterous toddler in the supermarket, and exchanging a sympathetic glance;

- a teacher's delighted response to a student's sudden grasp of something which had been difficult to understand;

- walking with someone you love in the countryside and smiling at each other, sharing the pleasure of the moment;

In all of these situations the people involved share their inner responses without fear of being discounted or rejected.

These are the ways we structure our time to get strokes. Each of the categories provides strokes of varying value and we have our own ideal balance which helps us to feel our life is satisfying and productive.

> *Exercise: Make a 'Time-Structure Pie Chart' by drawing a circle. Divide the circle into slices representing the amounts of your typical day that you spend in the six different forms of time structuring.*
>
> *Decide whether you want to change the look of the chart, and if so draw your ideal. Write down how you will actually make the changes. What will you do to increase the time structure that you want to increase; what will you do to decrease the time structure that you want less of?*
>
> *Be aware each day how you are structuring time. It will give you good practice if you also watch how others structure theirs. If you are at a meeting or a party, for instance, notice what time structures are in use.*

This chapter has explained how contact and recognition are as much human needs as food and water. We have looked at some of the ideas from Transactional Analysis which show how we convert our need for physical contact into the need for attention – for strokes or slaps. You have had an opportunity to explore how you are structuring your time at the moment. All of the work so far in the book has been encouraging you to identify ways in which you might change how you are spending your time at the moment so that you feel more satisfied with life. In the next chapter we will consider how to go about making the changes.

4

THE IMPORTANCE OF GOALS

Goals are important because they reflect our purpose in life. If you are feeling that your life at the moment seems pointless and empty, maybe you have lost sight of what you wanted to make of it. Or perhaps the stresses and strains of everyday life have obscured your deeper purpose. This is an opportunity for you to take a step back and take a look at what you want and how you might get it. Taking responsibility for yourself, your condition and circumstances is an important factor in making more constructive use of your time. Try the following exercise:

> *Exercise: (1) Imagine that you are very old and you overhear your relatives talking to their friends about you. What would you want them to say about you and your life? Write down your thoughts on this.*
>
> *(2) What would you like to see written as your epitaph after your death?*

The answers to these questions help you realize how far you are achieving the kind of life which will satisfy you when you come to look back. The purpose of this chapter is to explore a practical way in which you can bring about your aims by setting goals.

Don't feel daunted by the size of the changes you want to make. Have you ever watched a baby learning to walk? It can take quite a while. One day the baby is crawling around and tries to stand up by hanging on to something, but as soon as it lets go of the prop, down it falls. Babies don't usually go into a state of depression if they can't walk the first time they try – what they usually do is keep on trying. Each time they try to balance and fall over, they have another go. And in the end they usually succeed. Learning to walk and then to talk are tremendous achievements. If you accomplished these changes, you have the potential to make other changes for yourself. The next exercise will help you to focus on the changes you have to make:

> *Exercise: Jot down a list of some changes that would lead to your feeling more satisfied with yourself or your life. At this point, don't worry about how to bring them about – this is an exercise in identification. What is important is that the changes COULD be brought about by you if you chose. Avoid anything that requires someone else to change (e.g. 'One change I would like is for George to stop criticizing me' is not acceptable; 'I would like to control my feelings more so that I don't become so defensive' is better.)*

Undermining Labels

As you list your future goals, make sure they are not dictated by negative messages which undermine your self-esteem. Examples might be 'I'm not clever enough to do this' or 'I know that people don't really like me'. Allowing these negative thoughts to influence your approach to the various problems of life is like sticking a label on yourself which defines what you are. It is worth considering where these labels have come from.

> *Exercise (part 1): Write down five criticisms you make of yourself.*

Now ask yourself these questions about each of the items you have written:
When did you first know this was true of you? If the answer to

this question is 'Since I was a child' or 'a very long time', then it's worth reviewing. Maybe you were like this when you were young – but perhaps you've changed; a long time has passed. Think about who first told you this about yourself. Perhaps they were wrong – after all adults don't always understand what's going on in a child's mind but they do make assumptions based on its behaviour.

For instance, suppose you've written 'I'm lazy' as one of your self-criticisms – it's possible that when you were growing up, the grown-ups around you called you lazy every time they thought you weren't active enough. Maybe you were sitting and thinking – after all when you're a child there's a lot to think about! You are seeing the world for the first time and there's a lot of working out to do. If you kept hearing that you were lazy, you may have decided to believe it.

In our early childhood, we have to assume that the adults know what they're talking about. Maybe you got the message early on that you were stupid. This can come over by the constant belittling of a child's thinking. For instance, little Susan proudly explains to Mother and Father that the clouds stay up in the sky because they've been glued there by God. Father pats her on the head and says, 'What a cute little thing you are'. Mother says, 'Don't be silly, that's not right at all.' It is true that Susan hasn't got the facts right, but the quality of the thinking is good. She has noticed something and made connections with other information she has. The response to her, however, might lead her to believe that she's stupid so she might as well stop thinking altogether. Or she might stop sharing her thoughts with anyone.

'What is the advantage to me of not changing?' This may seem a strange question, since you may feel that there could not possibly be any advantages. But, if there were no benefits, why would you be continuing to think, feel or behave in ways which you find unacceptable?

These unconscious advantages are like barriers we can put up to stop the possibility of change. Here are some very common examples:

- *The Academic barrier: e.g. I'm no good at spelling/adding up/languages.* Once you believe that you are unable to do something, it follows that it's a waste of time to do the hard work involved in mastering it. The truth probably is that if you were willing and able to spend the time in study you would be able to increase your ability. But it's also true that this might also involve you in tedious, time consuming, tiring effort. The label 'I'm too stupid' allows you to avoid the whole thing.

- *The Age Barrier: e.g. I'm too old/young to change.* Any change involves risk. You can't know in advance how anything you decide on will go. All you can know is that things won't be the same. This label means you never have to face the risks that go with change.

- *The Ethnic Barrier: e.g. I'm like this because I'm Jewish/ Black/Chinese.* Accepting ethnic stereotypical behaviour in yourself gives you a great reason to explain or justify behaviour which might cause a problem and would be difficult to change. For example, I remember a student who responded to being criticised as unpredictable and temperamental by saying, 'But I'm Latin American – that's how I am, I can't help it.'

- *The Incompetency Barrier: e.g. I'm careless/forgetful/clumsy.* These labels give a convenient excuse for not taking responsibility for keeping your agreements. Once you believe that's how you are, you won't have to work at things like being on time, remembering promises, taking care of those around you.

- *The Accident of Birth Barrier: e.g. I'm shy/anxious/aggressive/bad-tempered – just like my mother/father/Aunt Jane . . .* This label allows you to blame your parents or relatives for being the way you are. How can you be expected to change something which happened before you were born and anyway is the fault of someone else?

- *The History Barrier: e.g. I'm this way because I'm an only child/one of a big family/my parents divorced/we were so poor when I grew up . . .* It is true that our early history has a great impact on us. However it is not true that those early experiences have to continue to rule how you behave. Self-defeating behaviour can be challenged and changed. Nothing will correct an unhappy childhood – but the effect of the unhappiness doesn't have to be carried like a burden throughout life. Once again, the advantage is that you can blame someone else for the way you are behaving.

- *The Physiological Barrier: e.g. I'm too short/tall/ugly/dark/ fair ...* These labels are useful because they can provide a good reason for not taking the risks that go with making intimate relationships. They feed low self-esteem and once you believe that your physical appearance matters more than your personality, you can opt out of the whole risky business of making close relationships in which you can be vulnerable.

Do you identify with any of the above? If so, take this opportunity to resolve to liberate yourself from these barriers.

> *Exercise: (Part 2) Rewrite the items you listed in the first part of this exercise, preceding each statement with one of these phrases 'I used to think I was ...'; 'I choose to be ...'; 'From today I will no longer be ...'*

It's a Goal!

So how can you change? The first step is to decide on your goals. Before we take a careful look at what a goal actually is, let's consider what it isn't. Usually when we have identified a problem, we tell ourselves what we have to do to solve it. For example, Sue realized that she hadn't been feeling as energetic as she used to. She said 'I'm letting myself go; I realize I'm getting older but I do want to stay healthy.' Alec, after telling a counselling group meeting how unhappy he was feeling, realized that there were some ways in which he, himself, was contributing to his unhappiness. He said, 'I know that I could be in better control of my time at work. I tend to just let things happen and then I respond to them. So I'm often working late and when I get home, I'm too tired to take much notice of Sally and the children. I've got to take more control and change my priorities.'

Both Sue and Alec have identified a problem and want to do something about it. They have both stated their ambitions, but have you noticed that they haven't actually said how they are going to achieve the changes they want. The problem is that unless they clarify their ideas further, they may fail to make any substantial change, even though they have every intention of doing so. They have made resolutions in the same way that most of us do at the New Year. When we make these resolutions, we are sincere in wanting to make the changes come about but many of us fail to make them happen. The reason for our failure is usually that we state them too generally without really thinking through what we will actually do.

There is nothing wrong with ambitions; in fact they are often the first step to deciding on a programme of change. 'I'm going to get healthier'; 'I will have a more mature attitude'; 'I will be more assertive'; 'I want to do well at college' are all examples of fine aspirations but just talking about them won't achieve the necessary changes to bring them about.

If you don't define your goals clearly, you may be programming yourself to fail. There are several steps in the process of translating an ambition into an accomplishment.

The first step is to break down the ambition into a set of objectives. Objectives are more specific than ambitions. For instance, Sue's ambition is to get healthier. Objectives that would help accomplish her ambition might be 'going on a diet', 'taking more exercise'. Useful objectives for Alec would include 'spending less time on work', 'spending more time with the children', 'sharing the household chores'. You can see that each of these objectives is more concrete than the ambition, although, in themselves, they are not yet enough to ensure success.

> *Exercise: Write down one of your ambitions for change and if it is a very general statement, list any things you can think of which would help you towards accomplishing it. These are your objectives.*

The next step is to convert these objectives into goals. Goals are specific actions which will change the situation. For instance, Sue needs to spell out more precisely what she intends to do. One of her objectives might be to take more exercise. She could set herself the goal 'I will lose 12 lbs in weight by the end of the year'.

65

This goal is clear, specific and measurable. One of Alec's goals could be 'to spend half an hour playing with the children before their bedtime each evening'.

Goals need to be: Clear, specific, measurable: Setting goals is a meaningless exercise if you don't know when and how much you have succeeded. Each statement should spell out exactly what you hope to accomplish and when you intend to accomplish it by. One sign that your goal is concrete and specific enough is that it can be measured. It's easy to think that these kind of things can't be measured, but finding a clear-headed way to calculate your progress may mean all the difference between success and failure.

Here are some points which will help you determine how you are succeeding:

What is the starting point? You need to be clear about what is actually happening now and precisely how you want things to be different. Sue has decided she is overweight and wants to do something about it. Before beginning a diet she weighs herself and finds that her weight is 150 lbs. According to the charts she should be around 120 lbs. For a month she keeps a food journal, noting down everything she eats and recording the calories. She continues to weigh herself and at the end of the month, she still weighs 150 lbs but now she knows the average number of calories she is getting each day. This is her starting point, and she can set a goal knowing just how much she needs to reduce her calorie intake to reach her desired weight. Find your starting point by asking:

How much? Quantity is an important factor.

- 'This week, I've brought work home four evenings in a row.'
- 'I lost my temper three times today.'
- 'I've been smoking thirty-five cigarettes a day.'
- 'every month, since I've had this job, my money has run out before my next pay cheque is due.'

How good? Quality is the next consideration.

- 'I'm too tired at the end of the day to pay attention to my family.'
- 'I feel out of breath whenever I walk up stairs.'
- 'I'm lonely and bored in the evenings because I don't have any close friends.'

What are you gaining and losing? It is important to identify any benefits you gain from what is happening now, so that those needs can be fulfilled some other way. What price are you paying for your present behaviour?

- 'I get the job done but I feel guilty because I am putting that over and above my need to be with the family.'
- 'I love sweet things; when I'm feeling low they are really comforting but I am putting on weight.'
- 'I don't want to break up my marriage but I feel so trapped and unhappy.'

Make sure that any goal you set provides you with benefits which outweigh the costs, otherwise the price will seem too high. This is why it is so useful to be able to measure the goal in some way.

When you've determined your starting point consider the following:

Is my Goal Practical?: Ambitions can be very grand and idealistic. Goals are much more down-to-earth; it's pointless to set goals which are beyond your resources. For instance some goals would be impractical because you don't yet have the life skills to succeed. If this is the case, you will need some goals to help you gain the necessary skills or knowledge. Limitations in your environment also have to be considered.

Is It Sufficient?: Not only can goals be set too high; they can also be set too low. Effective goals need to have some muscle, otherwise the whole process will become tedious. If the goals you carry out don't make some substantial difference, you will begin to feel that the effort is just not worthwhile. This doesn't mean that goals which are easy to achieve should be ruled out. Setting goals in which you can succeed is a big motivator – each success brings you a step closer to your ambition.

What's the Value?:   Each goal you set should fit in with your own set of values. We've probably all been in the situation where someone gives us some advice as to how we can solve a problem or be a better person. We know the advice itself is sensible but somehow we just don't get around to trying it. The likelihood is that this particular suggestion does not fit in with our own set of values. We all have a set of values, ideas of what is right and wrong and this framework is highly influential in determining how we respond. For instance, if one of Alec's values is committing himself to attaining success in his job, his feeling of self-esteem will depend on how much he sees himself to be achieving this success. This in turn leads him to direct more and more time and energy towards work and less towards his family. In order to change, he may need to think hard about his present value system and decide on its wisdom.

Is It Under My Control?:   Check that the goals you are setting don't depend on the co-operation of other people for their success.

A Success Story

Delia was not very happy with her life. She had no really close friends and often felt left out on social occasions. Her ambition was to have a better social life and make some friends. She decided that one way to bring people closer to her would be to show more interest in them. As she explored her starting point, she realized that to a large extent it was her own behaviour which prevented other people getting close. She realized that one of her big fears was of being rejected. In fact, her fear of rejection was so strong she had unconsciously decided not to give anyone the chance. She was telling herself 'If you don't let anyone close, they can't reject you.' This of course is true, and so the benefit for her was that she didn't risk the unhappiness of rebuff; however the cost was clear. She felt lonely and unfulfilled.

The message she was giving herself resulted in behaviour which made her appear cold and distant towards others, so that they didn't feel invited towards her. Once she became conscious of this process she decided that one of her objectives would be to show more interest in people by becoming a better listener.

People respond to attentive listening very positively. If she showed more interest in other people they would feel warmer towards her and she would stand more chance of making lasting friendships.

One goal that she felt would help her accomplish this was to practise reflecting back what people said to her as a way of checking that she understood them. She joined a counselling group so that she could practise the skills she wanted to develop. This is the way she stated her goal: 'I will reflect back, in my own words, what someone says in the group [*clear, specific*] at least three times [*measurable*] in each meeting. I want to do this for four weeks and then I will begin to practise outside the group. I'd like to be able to report back how I'm getting on.' She prizes this goal because it will prove to her that she is able to get over her anxiety about being rejected. She feels it is practical and sufficient as a start. She also knows where she wants this gentle beginning to lead.

Of course this goal on its own won't solve all Delia's problems; nevertheless you can see how it is a step towards her taking responsibility for changing her way of relating to people. As she succeeds and gets positive feedback from the group she will begin to see her fears in perspective. To a child, abandonment is life-threatening. When we are grown-up this isn't really the case. It is true that the more intimate a relationship, the greater the vulnerability. It's also true that rejection is not the same thing as total destruction. Delia can learn that taking the risk is less costly than protecting herself against the fantasy that life would end if she was forsaken by a friend.

Exercise: Here is a structure to help you set goals which will help you accomplish the change you want to make:

My ambition is _____

Objectives that would help me reach my ambition:

1 _____

2 _____

3 _____

The objective I will work on first is:

_____

One goal which will help me is:

_____

_____

_____

Now check that your goal is properly stated by going through the following set of questions:

My goal is/isn't clear and specific

I can/can't measure the goal

The goal is/isn't practical bearing in mind my present resources.

The goal is/isn't sufficient to make a difference to the present situation

I value this goal because_____

The time frame I have set myself is/isn't reasonable

What Happens Next?

Your next step is to decide just how to achieve your goals. This is where your creativity and imagination will help you most. The more possibilities you can generate, the better. If you only have one course of action and that proves too difficult, you are really stuck. Having several choices allows you to be flexible in your approach. If the first one doesn't work, you can move on to your second without feeling that the whole enterprise is a failure.

The following stories demonstrate how creative thinking can be extremely useful in making plans for achieving your goals.

Geoffrey wants to be a teacher but he didn't get the A levels he needed to enter university. When he got his results he said to himself, 'Well, that's it. I'm just not clever enough; I'll never be a teacher and whatever I do will be second best.' He eventually got a job in a college as a technical assistant. He enjoyed being in the college atmosphere, but never really felt satisfied.

Bernard also had ambitions to teach, and also failed to get the A levels he needed. His attitude was different though. He discussed the situation with a careers counsellor who helped him see various possibilities. He could continue full-time study in the sixth form and try the exams again; he could leave school and study part-time; he could take a break from study altogether; he could give up the idea of teaching and explore other career possibilities and so on. He decided to take a break and got accepted on a volunteer scheme in which he travelled to an underdeveloped country to work for a year. He found himself in a village where, as well as undertaking manual work, he helped with teaching English to the children at school. The year's break gave him a valuable opportunity to review his goals and in fact confirmed his commitment to teaching. His outlook on life widened as he met and worked with many different types of people. When he returned to England, he found work as a waiter and retook his A levels. This time he passed and was able to enter university. He is now a teacher working with children with special needs and gets a great deal of job satisfaction. His willingness to find other ways of working towards what he wanted stood him in good stead. The process took him longer than the traditional route he had first envisaged although on looking back he feels his first failure was the catalyst for valuable self-development.

To increase your creativity:

- *Look on the bright side:* Everyone knows about the difference between the optimist and the pessimist. One sees a glass as half full and the other as half empty. It is very hard to generate new thinking if you feel depressed and power-less; so try to think about your problems as opportunities for change rather than barriers.

- *Accept that life is not perfect:* Wanting your life to be as good as possible is one thing, seeking perfection is something else! Looking for perfection in everything will dampen your creativity. People, for instance, cannot be perfect. If you are only going to be satisfied by faultlessness, you will con-stantly be disappointed. If you are trying to be the perfect mother, lover, partner you will often be beset by doubts and feelings of inadequacy. In these cases it would be more sen-sible to work out what would be 'good enough'.

- *Think flexibly:* Every time you believe something abso-lutely, you can't allow yourself any leeway in how you approach it. Take time to examine your own set of beliefs and check whether they are appropriate. This is like turning out your wardrobe. There will be some clothes which fitted you once but are now out-of-date or so unsuitable you can't think why you bought them in the first place; these you will want to dispose of. Some clothes don't quite fit now but with a little adjustment would be quite wearable. Then there are the ones which you know you like and will continue to wear. Each time you throw out an unsuitable garment, you have room for something new. You can examine your belief system in the same way, discarding beliefs which are no longer appropriate and making way for more flexible think-ing.

Examples of self-defeating beliefs:

- I must be loved or liked by everyone.
- It is always easier to avoid facing difficulties than to deal with them.
- Disagreement and conflict should always be avoided.
- It is not going to be possible for me to change because people cannot change.
- A person is either totally good or totally bad. If they are good I have to accept everything about them – if they are bad I have to reject everything about them.

- People are too fragile to be faced with the truth.
- Having problems which I can't resolve means I am weak and incompetent.
- There is only one right way to deal with a situation.

- *Be curious.* Get into the habit of questioning almost everything. When you were a child your curiosity helped you to understand and test out your world. It is so easy to lose this sense of curiosity as we grow up and have to face all the problems, but this desire to understand everything is a great source of creativity and well worth cultivating.

- *Broaden your interests:* As you think about how you are using your time at the moment you may become aware that your range of interests is narrow. Maybe all your energy is put into your work or maybe you spend most of your leisure time passively. The more varied your interests are, the more you will stimulate your creativity.

- *Don't be afraid of your fear:* Fear is a natural reaction to change, but it can be constructive or destructive. You can use it constructively to protect you from taking dangerous risks. You can decide how real your fears are by exploring the changes you contemplate; by working out as far as possible the likely effects; by taking sensible protective measures and so on. Or you can allow the fear to take over and rule your reaction. Be clear where your fear is coming from. Is it a reaction to the assumptions you are making about the future? Many of us tend to think in disaster scripts. We see ourselves putting the change we want into action and then immediately create a picture in our mind of all the disasters that could happen. We end up alone, rejected, despised, a laughing stock ... Then our body, sensibly enough, reacts to this thinking and creates the familiar paralysis of fear. However – the whole thing is a fantasy since we cannot know what is going to happen.

- *Do something different:* Identify the repetitive patterns in your life and resolve to change how you are reacting. We all have our own particular ways of approaching problems and continue to try to solve them by doing whatever we are doing, but harder. But if it isn't working now – it's probably not going to work however hard you try. So do something different.

Brainstorming. An excellent way of generating creative ideas for action is brainstorming. This idea is used extensively in business and is great fun and very effective. The point is to generate as many ways of achieving a goal as possible. Although you can do it as a personal exercise on your own, it works very well when you get together with a few other people. They need not know very much about your particular problem and don't have to be experts. In fact there are certain advantages to having a completely naive response because our familiarity with the situation tends to keep us within the restrictions of our predictable thinking patterns. There are certain rules, however, that have to be kept:

1 *Set the scene:* Explain what you are trying to achieve in very simple terms. e.g. 'I'm aiming to stop smoking by the end of the summer'; 'I intend to stop taking work home at weekends'; 'I want to lose twelve pounds in weight'; 'My goal is to get help with the washing up at least three times a week'.

2 *Explain the rules:* Everyone will give their ideas as to what you could do but at this point there will be no discussion or criticism given on the ideas. Tell people that you want to hear wild and fantastic ideas as well as sensible and practical suggestions. Encourage them to let themselves go, the longer the list, the more likelihood of finding fruitful ideas. Write down every suggestion, even those which may seem quite impractical.

3 *Explore possibilities:* When people run out of steam, go through the list. Take each item and mark 'yes' against any items you feel are practical possibilities and 'no' for anything you are not willing to consider under any circumstances. There may be some items on the list which as they stand are not practical but could have the germ of an idea in them. Mark these with 'M' for maybe. At this point

you don't have to reject an idea because you can't see how to do it – you never know, there may be a way!

Gavin wanted to stop smoking as one of his goals towards improved health. He organized a brainstorming session with a group of friends and came up with this list, which he marked:

- Stop immediately. (M)
- Stop gradually. (Yes)
- Join a group of people all of whom want to stop smoking. (M)
- Use one of the drug-based remedies being advertised. (No)
- Start chain-smoking so you just get fed up with it. (No)
- Go into counselling and find out the reasons why you smoke. (M)
- Wear a big badge that says 'I am trying to stop, so don't offer or sell me any cigarettes.' (Yes)
- Visit a lung cancer ward. (M)
- Tell everyone you want to stop. (Yes)
- Only smoke half a cigarette then put it out. (No)
- Avoid being with people who smoke. (M)
- Every time you want a cigarette, eat something you like. (Yes)
- Every time you want a cigarette, do something you like. (Yes)
- Save the money and spend it on a treat. (Yes)
- Find something else to do with your hands. (Yes)
- Ask people what they think about passive smoking. (M)
- Throw away all the cigarettes you have at the moment. (No)

He combined some of the 'yeses' and came up with a plan to cut down the number of cigarettes he smoked each week until by the third week he had stopped altogether. He liked the idea of the badge and wore it. He told everyone what he was doing because he knew that he wouldn't want to lose face by failing. He carried peppermints around with him and used them to help spin out his daily 'allowance' of cigarettes. He also began keeping the money he saved by not smoking so much and at the end of each week bought himself a book or a tape so that he could see the results.

He kept some of the other suggestions to fall back on if his first plan failed.

75

> *Exercise: Take one of the goals which you have set*
> *yourself and brainstorm a list of possible ways of*
> *achieving it. If you want to involve other people, ex-*
> *plain to them what you want from them and then*
> *list all the suggestions they make. Don't evaluate*
> *any of the suggestions until the list is complete,*
> *then go through it marking each item with 'yes',*
> *'no' or 'm'.*

The next stage is to create a plan of action to help you turn your thinking into reality. The following considerations will help you decide on your plan of action:

Who or what could help: When you have set your goal and decided on a possible course of action, it is useful to ask yourself how you could get help. For instance, are there any *people* who could help? Do you know of anyone who has succeeded with a similar goal? Do you know anyone who may have some useful information for you? Is there anyone who could teach you a skill that would help?

Are there any *places* that could help? Would it be useful to visit a library to get some information? Could you get some inspiration from a church or a quiet place for meditation?

Are there any *things* that would help you? Is there a book, for instance, that could give you information or guidance? Some gadget which would make life easier? Particular food supplements which might energise you?

Are there any *organisations* that could help you? For instance, are there any self-help groups where people with similar problems meet to support each other.

Making a Decision

Sometimes, the thing that holds you up from making progress as quickly as you could is the difficulty of making a choice between options open, especially when there is no one solution which seems ideal. Here are some approaches which can help you to make progress:

The Balance Sheet   Decisions always carry gains and losses like a balance sheet. Caroline and John, for instance, are expecting their first baby. Caroline is considering the pros and cons of continuing to work or becoming a full-time mother. Her balance sheet looks like this:

Potential Gains from Leaving Work:

For me: I would be able to devote all my energies to the child. I would be able to make good contacts with other mothers. I think I will be a good mother and I want to feel fulfilled in that role.

- *Positive for me:* because I want to feel that I am providing the baby with a secure and consistent environment. I always like to feel that I am doing my best in whatever I do and I'd like to enjoy being a mum.

- *Negative for me:* because I'm afraid that I might get bored and resentful being at home. I might feel envious towards John because of his continuing to be in the working world.

For John: John will benefit because I will be taking responsibility for the day-to-day care of the baby. He will be able to continue his career.

- *Positive for me:* because I know his career is important to him.

- *Negative for me:* because our interests will be so different and we might become very distant from each other. Our relationship might suffer.

Potential Costs of Leaving Work:

For me: I would miss the intellectual challenge of working as well as the independence of earning an income. It might be easy to become very bored and resentful at home with a small child. We will also have much less money and have to economize.

- *Positive for me:* because although we will have less money, I know that we can manage and I think I will enjoy the challenge of managing on less. Although I'd miss work, I could keep up by reading and also begin to explore other areas.

- *Negative for me:* because I might begin to feel lonely and it might be more difficult to manage than I think.

For John: He would have the responsibility of being the main breadwinner.

- *Positive for me:* because this could be a time for me to re-evaluate what I want to do with my life and how I might want to work in the future.

- *Negative for me:* because he might get resentful at having less opportunity to be involved with the baby.

John also made his balance sheet and they each discussed the costs and benefits they felt would affect them and each other. This process allowed them to feel they made their decision carefully and responsibly on the basis of minimizing the costs and maximizing the benefits. When they hit problems, they were able to discuss what was happening without blaming each other for lack of care or thought.

Cost Benefit Rating: A variation on the theme is to give each cost and benefit a rating to help you choose between different options. Derek is unhappy with his progress in his present job. He feels stuck at his present level but knows that in the present economic climate it may not be wise to leave his present firm. He writes out his options – for example:

- to wait for promotion in the present job;

- to seek a more senior job in a similar department in another company;

- to change direction and try for a transfer to another department in the present company.

He then writes the first option at the top of the sheet of paper, divides the page down the middle and heads the column on the left Costs and that on the right Benefits. He then lists the various costs and benefits as he sees them and gives each one a score on a 1–10 scale. 1 for very slight and 10 for major advantages or disadvantages:

Option: Waiting for Promotion

COSTS	RATING	BENEFITS	RATING
No change of scene	3	Low stress	5
Lack of challenge	7		
		I won't need to move house	6
Promotion might not come	9		
Competing with other staff	8		
		I'm well-known in the company	2
I know I can do the job	8		

His 'costs' score is 27 and the 'benefit' score is 21. As he goes through this exercise with each option he will be able to clarify the comparative costs and benefits of possible actions. He can also determine which costs are acceptable. If there is no option which is clearly better than any other he will have to choose either (a) to postpone the decision or (b) risk choosing one option even though there may be no convincing factor.

Here is how you can use this idea:

1 Identify your options.

2 Draw up a sheet of paper as described with Cost and Benefit columns. Write the first option at the top of the page and list the costs and benefits. Give each a rating on the 1–10 scale.

3 Put a circle round the two biggest disadvantages and the two biggest advantages.

4 Repeat process for each option.

5 Place your cost/benefit sheets alongside each other. Think about and/or talk through your reactions to each sheet.

6 Check to see whether any option seems on balance to give you most of what you want. If it does, decide whether the costs of it are acceptable to you. If so, start!

7 If there is no option which is clearly better for you than another then you have to choose either (a) to postpone the decision or (b) risk choosing an option without a convincing factor.

8 It is useful to think through 'What happens if I do nothing or fail to make a decision?' Doing nothing is an option which it might be productive to consider in exactly the same way as the other options.

Helping/Hindering Forces   Another approach identifies the external and internal forces which might help or hinder options. This is sometimes called a force-field analysis and is a way of improving your chances of achieving an objective or an action plan. It means examining what is involved in the changes you want to make and identifying which forces may be helpful or which may work against the change.

Simon, for instance, is lonely and finds it very difficult to make relationships with the opposite sex. He has set some goals to increase his social life and has picked joining a singles club as a possibility from the brainstorming exercise.

He has identified all the restraints which could hold him back and made them into a list of hindering forces:

- lack of money;

- fear;

- don't know where to find one;

- people will think I can't make it on my own;

- I've heard they have a bad reputation;

- I've never done it before;

- shyness.

Having thought about all the constraints, Simon then made a list of forces which could help him:

- I really do want to meet people;

- I know someone who goes to a singles club and could ask them how to go about it;

- there are magazines which advertise singles clubs;

- I do feel excited about doing something to change things;

- I'm willing to try it at least once;

- other people there will be like me;

- it's a good way to meet people without having to make a commitment.

He draws a diagram representing the forces working for and against the option of joining a singles club.

HINDERING FORCES

Lack of money	Fear	Don't know where to find one	People will think I'm a failure	Never done it before	I'm too shy

HELPING FORCES

Strong desire to meet people	I will feel more in control of my life	Information from magazines	People will be in the same position as me	Exciting to do something new	Easy way to meet people without commitment

The diagram makes the problem almost physical. One of the laws of physics is that if the forces operating on an object in a state of equilibrium are increased in one direction, then the forces in the opposite direction must increase equally if the equilibrium is to be maintained.

One way of using this idea is to consider each force carefully, weakening the negative and strengthening the positive. To do this you need to identify ways in which you can reduce, minimize or eliminate (although not annihilate) each force working against you. And then work out how to increase, strengthen or maximize each positive force.

Here is how you can apply this technique:

1 Identify your objective. Work on one objective at a time.

2 List the forces working in favour of what you want to achieve. (A positive force is anything which will contribute to your achieving your objective). Be very specific in listing the forces and remember they may come from inside or outside you. Indicate how the force will contribute to your achieving what you want.

3 List all the forces working against you. Again, be specific

and list all factors, internal and external, which will work against you. Describe the effect you think each will have on your achieving your objective.

4 Analyse the forces by identifying which are most important. Check that they are *real* rather than assumed and that they will have a significant effect on whether or not you succeed. Circle all the important forces on your lists. Check whether you need any extra information about any of the forces you have identified.

5 Weaken the negative; strengthen the positive. Work on each in turn. If you really cannot find a way of reducing the pressure of a particular force, write, 'no possible action' against it.

6 Assess how possible your objective or plan of action now seems and ask yourself:

Do the positives clearly outweigh the negatives? If the answer is 'yes' ask yourself again: 'Do I really want to achieve this?' If the answer is 'no', then your choice is to abandon it or change it. It might, for instance, be possible to modify the original by lowering your sights or increasing the target time.

This chapter has taken you through a range of ideas for thinking through the practicalities of making changes in yourself or your lifestyle. Next we will explore turning the theory into practice.

5

TIME FOR ACTION

The theme of this chapter is action. Taking action can be an effective antidote to many of the barriers we have already explored such as depression, anxiety, stress, fear, worry and guilt. All of these states contribute to the feeling of powerlessness which in turn leads to immobility.

Before we get on to the practicalities of making action plans that work, check that you aren't falling into two very common thinking traps which are likely to sabotage your success.

There's Really Nothing I Can Do! Once you've said this to yourself, you have effectively stopped yourself from progressing. You have sentenced yourself to remaining in the same situation. Say instead to yourself, 'Although I'm not at all sure what to do, I'm convinced there must be something. I'm not going to be controlled into doing nothing.' Thinking in this way will at least help you to gather energy to counteract your feelings of listlessness and gloom. At its best it will lead to creative solutions, but even if it doesn't you will be developing a new habit of approaching life actively and making the best possible use of your time whatever the circumstances.

That's Just the Way Things Are! This is the second great saboteur. It is the resignation that comes from the belief that because things are as they are now, they can never be changed. You only have to consider the changes in society in the past fifty years to know that this idea is quite wrong. In the 1920s and 30s people never dreamed of things which are commonplace for us; easy air travel to all parts of the globe; computers which take seconds to carry out calculations which were not even possible then; cures for diseases which seemed inevitable killers and so on. You can effect changes in much smaller ways. For instance, suppose you are getting very frustrated by having to wait in a slow supermarket queue, you can shrug your shoulders and say to yourself, 'There's no way I can do anything about this. This is just the way things have to be.' This thought guarantees that you will continue to feel frustrated. Suppose you thought, 'Hang on a minute. I don't have to put up with this. I'm a customer and this store depends for its existence on people like me. I'm not just going to stand here, I'm going to do something.' All sorts of possibilities now open up for you. You could find the manager and ask him or her to open up more check-outs; if you don't get any co-operation you could refuse to wait and leave your trolley in the queue with a note on it to say why you didn't wait; you could tell the manager that you do not intend to continue shopping in this store and that you will write to the head office to explain why; you could even move to the head of the queue and help unload the baskets to speed things up; you could persuade other customers to complain. These actions may or may not change the supermarket's efficiency but any of them will certainly make you feel more active and less powerless.

Easy as ABC:

How to prioritise your goals is an important consideration if there are many changes you would like to make.

The following exercise is to help you decide where to start. You will put your goals in order of importance so that you can make a realistic plan for the long- and short-term.

> *Exercise: In previous chapters you have made lists of the changes you want to make in your life. Refer now to those lists or make a new one. Examples could include move to a new home, lose weight, take a holiday, earn more, stop smoking, communicate better with family, be more patient, get out of debt, change jobs and so on.*

Now divide them into four lists. The first are those things you want to accomplish in the next five years; the second those things you want to accomplish in the next year; the third those things you want in the next six months and finally the list for the coming month.

Go over the four lists and classify each item as A, B and C priority. A items are those things which you feel are most important, and are essential to achieving your ambitions. B items can be put off for a while; they may be items which would be useful but not vital to your most important ambitions. They may be things which have a kind of maintenance function so that you can be free to work on the changes you want to make. C are those items which don't really contribute to your most crucial aspirations; perhaps they are on your list because someone else thinks you ought to do them or maybe they are unnecessary time-stealers.

Choose two A items from each category (five-year, one-year, six-month and one-month). Write these down under the heading 'My most important priorities'.

The point of this exercise is to enable you to identify those areas on which you should work first.

There is one more step you can take before committing yourself to a plan of action.

Exercise: Imagine you have just been told by your doctor that you have one year to live. You won't ex-perience any discomfort or disability during this time and so you will be able to do anything you can do at the moment. Now write the list of goals for this last year of your life.

If this list differs from your previous list, take some time to think about what this might mean. Maybe the second list is a more truthful picture of your wants and needs. Perhaps you can make up a third list which is a mixture of both.

A Plan of Action. So now you know how to set goals and have identified the best place to start. The next step is to make a plan of action. This means planning your time. Good planning will help you direct your energy towards achieving your major goals. You wouldn't, after all, start out on a journey in an unknown territory without a map. Your plan of action will be your map and will guide you through the landscape of change.

There are many ways of approaching making a plan. Whichever method you evolve, write it down or record it on a tape. Once you have committed your thoughts to paper or tape they are harder to forget, ignore or avoid.

> *Exercise (Part 1): Take a large sheet of paper and draw a circle to represent a month. Divide the circle into segments representing your main activities (e.g. child care, work, sleep, eating, study, leisure etc.) Taking your list of goals, write them in whichever segment they fall.*

If you have goals which mean you will be spending time on something which you don't do at the moment, make space for it. Each time you add something, you will of course need to decide where you will take the time from. This is an important part of the process as it prevents you creating an unrealistic time plan.

> *Exercise (Part 2): Take a new sheet of paper and draw a circle to represent a typical week. Once again divide the circle into segments, and place your goals in the appropriate segment.*

Make sure that your circle includes time for play, especially if you are the kind of person who feels guilty if you find yourself having fun rather than furthering your goals. Giving yourself time for recreation is important. If you only spend money from your bank account without replacing it – it will finally run out. Similarly, if you expend mental or physical energy without giving yourself time to replace or recreate it – it will run out. You could end up feeling too tired to put in the effort of maintaining your goals. More about this in Chapter 7.

The previous exercise gives you a general sense of the shape of your time and how your new goals can fit in. The next step is to allocate your actual time. You will need to buy or make a diary that gives a whole page to a day. Schedule your time to take account of what you want to achieve. Make a time plan for each day.

'To Do' or 'Not To Do':

A useful technique to help you keep focused on important goals is to keep a daily 'To Do Today' list. Break your larger goals into very small, short-term goals. As you take each of these small steps, you will get an important sense of accomplishment and momentum.

Your 'To Do' list will include the small, short-term goals you want to accomplish for a particular day. You can use the A, B and C system for these daily lists. If you find yourself spending a lot of time on a C item when A items have not been tackled, you are either wasting time or have not given the task a sufficient priority. Work your way down from the A items to the C items.

Review your progress at the end of each week. You will soon find out how realistic your planning is and you may need to adjust your timetable. If you find that you are constantly writing in a goal which somehow just doesn't get done, you need to think about what is happening. Check against the criteria in Chapter 4; perhaps it isn't specific, practical or substantial enough; maybe although it seems worthy it doesn't actually fit into your own value system. Or the problem may lie earlier in the process and you need to consider your analysis of the situation. You might notice that you have your favourite ways of avoiding undertaking goals. Like, for example, deciding that your desk needs tidying before you make a difficult phone call; or that you have to finish the book you are reading before going to the gym; or getting so tired that you have no energy for talking to someone about something important. In this case a 'Not To Do' list is just as important as the 'To Do' list. Write down all the avoidance strategies that steal your time, so that if you find yourself doing any of them you can check whether you really want to continue.

Can Someone Else Do It? In the business world, managers are expected to delegate work to those around them. As you become your own time manager, you too can consider this possibility. Getting others to help you frees you to concentrate on your main goals. Relationships can be improved by contact and communication.

For instance, Vicky had started an Open University Course as part of her plan to improve her qualifications. Up until then she had been responsible for child care, housework and general family maintenance. She discussed the situation with her partner, Joseph, and the children. They worked out a plan for more of the domestic chores to be taken over by others in the family. Joseph agreed to take over the cooking three times a week and the children agreed to do domestic jobs for increased pocket money. This allowed Vicky the time she needed to concentrate on her study and had the unexpected reward of bringing the family closer together. It's not that they were unhappy before, but while Vicky had taken responsibility for the domestic side of their life Joseph and the children did not need to be involved. Now they were all part of the plan of action and needed to discuss it whenever there were problems.

Are there people around you – a partner, children, friends who would be willing to give you a hand? Is there a chance that you could employ someone to take on tasks which eat up your time? If employing someone is not a possibility, is there some exchange you can make?

One of Julia's ambitions was to be more creative and an objective she felt would help her achieve this was to learn to draw and paint. She had always enjoyed art at school but she never seemed to have any time to develop this now. Since leaving school she had worked as a hairdresser and her spare time was taken up with her social life and keeping her flat in good order. She went through the exercise of setting goals and making an action plan. One of her goals was to join a local art class. Her time log showed that all her free time was taken up with housework, shopping, meeting friends and so on. Much of the housework came into the B group activities. She didn't particularly enjoy it but it had to be done because she would hate the flat to be untidy and dirty. She didn't want to give up the time she spent with her friends. She thought about delegating the housework but couldn't think of anyone who would volunteer to do it for her! She couldn't afford to pay current rates for domestic help. She was discussing this with her friend, Sally, who said that she would be willing to do Julia's housework once a week if Julia would look after her hair in return. Thus, Julia got time for her art class; the housework got done; Sally's hair never looked better!

> *Exercise: Look over your ABC list and make a note of any items which could be done by someone else. These would probably be B and C items. Now make a list of all the possible people in your life who might be willing and able to take on some of the tasks. Make a note as to the payment or exchange each might require.*

At this point you might be thinking, 'That's all very well, but . . .' Take a moment to put your 'Buts' under the spotlight.

'BUT I couldn't trust anyone to do it as well as I can': This is not a good reason for continuing to do a B priority yourself. Would the world really come to an end if your high standards were not maintained? The question is, will the person to whom you have delegated do it well enough?

'BUT supposing mistakes are made?' By giving clear instructions and being available and approachable, you can reduce your anxiety about mistakes.

'BUT I don't like asking people to do things' There is a myth that to be really successful you ought to be able to manage everything yourself and that to ask for help is a weakness. In fact, knowing your limits and being able to make clear decisions about how you want to spend your time is strength. Don't assume that because a particular task is not very enjoyable or important to you, no one else likes it either. What may be a mundane, boring task to you might well give someone else a great deal of satisfaction.

'BUT I'll lose control' Well, yes. But do you need to be in control of absolutely everything, all the time?

'BUT I could do it quicker myself' That may be true in the first

instance, because you may have to give instructions and check on progress. But in the long run, nothing is quicker than not having to do it at all.

If you do decide to enlist help by delegating work to someone, here are some guidelines:

1. Work out the time needed to do the task and the time required to instruct or explain it.

2. Give clear, simple instructions and deadlines. If you want the other person to take responsibility up to a certain point, make that clear.

3. Check that the other person understands what you are asking for; that they are clear about what you want to achieve. Make sure, too, that they know what you are prepared to give in return.

4. Follow up to see how things are going. Be careful how you do this. The skill here is that the person should feel neither harassed nor abandoned.

5. Give the person feedback while the task is going on or when the task is finished. Check which they would prefer. Some people like to be left alone to get on with the job, others like to have regular opportunities to check they are doing OK. The following is a good formula: 'WHAT I would like done is . . .; this is HOW I would like it done . . .; I would like it done BY . . .; We are doing it BECAUSE . . . These are the areas you are free to decide . . .; these are the areas which I want you to discuss with me if you want to change . . .'

Doing More Than One Thing At A Time   One very creative way of managing time is to combine the information from the various exercises you have done so far. Christopher is a sales representative. His log showed that he spent up to three hours travelling each day to work and between appointments. One of his ambitions was to retire to France and he wanted to improve his fluency in French. He had tried evening classes but often missed them because he was too tired or got home too late.

To increase his enjoyment of driving he listened to music on the car's tape deck. He saw an advertisement for a taped language course and realized that he could capitalize on driving time to help him improve his French. His goal was to listen to the French tapes for half an hour a day while he was driving. By doing this he gradually built up his vocabulary and was able to practice in the privacy of the car.

Is there any hidden time in your time log? Time which you spend on repetitive tasks like ironing, preparing meals, driving or train travel; or time spent waiting in doctors' surgeries, restaurants, hairdressers and so on. Discovering this time can be a gift. Goals such as study, reading, writing letters, learning to relax can all be worked on at times like these.

Making the Day Plan Making the day plan is the key to feeling in control of your time. It is the next step from the 'To-Do Today' list because it tells you *when* you will carry out the various tasks. How you structure it is a personal matter. The simplest method is to use an appointments diary and write in each hour or so what you intend to do. A good time to do this is just before you go to bed. You can review what you accomplished during the day and decide on the best plan for tomorrow. Or you may prefer to do this as the first task of the morning. You may decide to write a general weekly plan and review it each day. Design your plan so that it guides you through the day helping you feel you are making the best possible use of your time. Make sure that it is related to your ambitions, objectives and goals. From time to time programme in a review to see how you are progressing with each goal.

Any Other Business This is an item on every agenda. It's there because unscheduled matters often crop up and this gives space for them. However carefully you plan your day, you can't predict everything. So schedule time in your day plan for interruptions and unforeseen problems. If they don't occur and everything goes to plan, you will have extra time. If they do, you won't feel pressured and out of control.

It is wise, also, to schedule some 'breathing spaces' for un-winding. There are several different ways you can organize this. For example, you can schedule a particular time each day, when you feel you most need it or when it is most appropriate. For some people, ten or fifteen minutes when they arrive home from work spent in quiet relaxation helps them to renew and focus their energy for the evening's activities. Make sure that anyone likely to interrupt you knows that you want to be left alone unless there is an emergency.

You might need to polish up your assertion skills to deal with unwanted telephone calls or visitors. Both can eat up time that you want for some special purpose.

Taking the Plunge

The theme of this chapter is moving from the theory of goal set-ting to actually doing what is necessary to effect the changes you want. It is a crucial but challenging step. Once you begin taking the actions required, things will change. You can't predict what will happen when change occurs and so it can be very frightening. Sometimes it can seem more comfortable to stay with the present situation which is at least familiar. It is often at this stage of the process that people find themselves stuck. The analysis has been done; areas for change identified; goals set; action plans made but nothing happens. It's like teetering on the edge of the swimming pool trying to get up the courage to jump in. Here is a very practi-cal idea to help you take the plunge into action.

> *Exercise: Make a checklist of questions to ask yourself before, during and after the action. The questions are to guide you along the way. They are intended as prompts so that you can avoid getting confused and losing the point of what you are try-ing to do, particularly if things don't go according to plan.*

For instance, suppose we go back to Caroline and John, from the previous chapter. Caroline has decided to continue working and is now considering the child care arrange-ments. She is about to begin interviewing people applying

93

for the job of looking after the baby. She has drawn up this checklist for herself:

Before: Am I clear what experience and qualities I am looking for? How will I ensure I get the information I need?

Am I clear about the relationship I want to exist between me and the carer?

Have I thought about the needs of the person taking the job?

Have I clarified the terms and conditions of employment?

During: Am I getting the information I need?

Am I listening carefully to the applicant?

Am I giving us time to communicate easily together?

What is my gut feeling? Why do I have that feeling?

Am I in control of the interview?

After: Am I satisfied with how I conducted the interviews?

Can I make a decision about the suitability of the various applicants?

Do I want to see any of them again?

If I am not happy with any of them, am I willing to continue this process until I find someone without getting impatient?

If I decide to offer the job, is there anything I want to add to or delete from the contract I am offering?

Obviously you have to design a check list which is helpful to you. If you are aware of any particular weak spots, make sure you include them in the list. Caroline was aware that she was likely to get impatient if she wasn't able to find someone fairly quickly. She included the question about being willing to continue if that happened, to remind her that she might regret making a quick decision.

Here are some questions that are generally useful:

Before: What is the worse thing that can happen? Am I prepared for that?

            Is this the only way of doing it?

            Am I clear about what I am expecting?

During: What am I thinking and feeling?

            What am I doing?

            Do I want to continue?

            Am I listening to the other person?

            What do I think the other person is thinking and feeling?

            Am I giving myself time to make a decision?

After: Am I satisfied with how things went?

            If not, what specifically would I want to change?

Not Enough Fun? Is this beginning to seem too organized and dreary? Are you afraid that with all these lists and plans the spontaneity will go out of your life? If you are feeling this way, take some time to think this through. You are reading this book because you want to take more control of your life and to make changes in how you spend your time. What I assume from that is that you are not entirely happy with how things are going at the moment. Rather than seeing activities like time logs, to-do lists, time plans and so on as restricting, try thinking about them as structures which will free you to use your time more satisfyingly.

Many of these techniques have been tried and tested in the business world where time is seen as a valuable resource. Using them for your personal life is like treating yourself as a business; the profit for you will be greater choice and control.

Summing Up

The main point of this chapter is how to get more in control of your time. Having a plan and working towards it is an important part of life. Here are some points to remember:

1 *Write it out:* Put your goals in writing. This is the way you turn your hopes and wishes into real possibilities.

2 *Be realistic:* Challenge yourself with your goals, but don't set yourself up to fail. If you've never climbed a mountain and set your first goal as reaching the summit of Everest by the end of next month, you won't be able to do it. Then you'll get frustrated and stop trying altogether.

3 *Have long-term ambitions but set short-term goals:* Succeeding in a goal you have set yourself is very rewarding and motivates you to continue. If your goals are too long-term you run the risk of feeling discouraged because you can't see any immediate progress.

4 *See yourself succeeding:* Imagine yourself as having achieved what you are setting out to do. You will have, of course, to do more than just think about what you want but don't underestimate the power of positive thinking.

5 *Be committed:* You do really have to *want* what you want. If you find that even though you have carefully followed all the suggestions given, somehow or other you never seem to achieve what you intend, check whether this is something you do really want for yourself. If you set goals to please others or because they are things you feel you *should* do

rather than *want* to do, you may not find it easy to achieve them.

> *Exercise: Choose one of the ambitions you have for yourself and imagine that you have achieved it. Give yourself time to picture yourself and your life now that you have made the changes you want. Let your imagination have full rein and allow yourself to experience the feelings that go with your success. Get into the habit of recalling these feelings while you are engaged in the process of changing.*

What Happens if Things Don't Go According to Plan?

It's possible that even though you do everything according to the book, things just don't go according to plan. If you find yourself in this position, DON'T GIVE UP! Give yourself a break and take some time to think through what's happening.

Reward yourself: First of all, before you start trying to work out what has happened, give yourself some reward for getting as far as you have. If you have never taken deliberate control of your life before and have worked through the goal-setting exercises – give yourself a pat on the back. Remember how a baby learns to walk and don't expect yourself to achieve major changes without any setbacks. When you have rewarded yourself, think through some of the following points.

Do you have a back-up plan? Having a contingency or back-up plan will stand you in good stead if something has got in the way of your achieving your original plan.

Have you lost sight of the wood for the trees? It is easy to get so involved in devising elaborate action plans that you get swamped in details and lose sight of your main goal.

What has actually happened? Don't get caught up in self-defeating thoughts and feelings because things haven't turned out the way you wanted. Think instead about what has actually happened. Evaluate the situation. If you are facing total failure, for instance, ask yourself the following questions: 'What's going wrong and what can be done to correct it?'; 'At what point did things start going wrong?'; 'Does the problem stem from something I am doing or from some external source?'

You may be having partial success. You may be making progress but not as completely, efficiently or quickly as you wanted. Ask yourself: 'What can I do to improve my plan?'; 'Does the problem lie with the goals I have set or with the plan I have made?'. 'Do I need to set further goals to help me along?'

Even if you have succeeded completely, it is worthwhile to evaluate the situation. Ask yourself: 'Where else in life can I use the strategies which have been so successful in this area?'. 'Can I use my learning to help others in the same situation?'

In this chapter we have explored various practical ways of turning your plans into action. In the following section we will look at how to say 'no' to things that are preventing you from taking more control of your time.

6

IT'S TIME TO SAY 'NO'!

One of the best time-saving decisions you could make is to say 'no' whenever it is safer or more sensible than saying 'yes'. This sounds so obvious and rational that you may wonder why a whole chapter is devoted to it. If you have never had any difficulty in refusing something you don't want, skip this chapter. On the other hand, continue reading if you ever feel resentful because:

- you seem to be so busy doing things for other people that you don't have time for yourself;

- people seem to take advantage of you;

- you often find yourself doing things you really don't want to do;

- you feel you are doing more than your share;

- you have to attend events or visit places where you don't really want to be;

- you agree to something because you don't want to hurt someone's feelings.

Most of us enjoy helping others but if we feel excessive demands are made on us it's easy to feel resentful.

> *Exercise: Make your own list of situations in which you find it difficult to give a refusal: (e.g. being asked to do something for someone when I'm*

obviously not very busy; being asked to lend money; a social invitation, etc). For some of us, it is not so much the actual situation which is the problem, but who it is who is asking. Some people seem much more difficult to refuse than others. List any people whom you find it hard to say 'no' to (e.g. my mother, my children, my boss, someone in an official position, etc) and finally make a list of times when you find it hard, (e.g. when I'm tired; when I'm in a hurry; when I think I'll be laughed at, etc).

Why is it so difficult for us to say 'no'? There seem to be a whole range of fears which come into play when we are faced with wanting to refuse someone. For instance:

- people might think that you are callous, uncaring, mean or selfish;
- if it's over something small you might be seen as petty and churlish;
- people will be hurt or offended;
- you'll lose people's respect;
- people won't like you;
- you won't be asked again.

Exercise: Still thinking about the situations you listed in the previous exercise, try to identify the fears that stopped you saying 'no'.

Identifying the fears behind any reluctance to say 'no' is the first step towards dealing with them. As you consider each one, you may realize that some of them are just not rational, perhaps because they developed in the past when you were a child. Others may be reasonable but you may want to re-examine any relationship which leaves you so much in the power of the other person. Some of the fears may be an accurate assessment of the situation and in these cases you can weigh up the risks and decide what you want to do.

How to Say 'No'

How you say 'no' is also important. Do you, for instance, find yourself padding out your refusal with lots of excuses or even lies like 'Of course I'd love to help out but I'm so busy I just can't see how I could manage it. Anyway, I really haven't been feeling so well lately,' or 'Well, you know that I would like nothing better than to look after her, but the children just won't let me do it.' On the other hand, you might refuse in such a way that the other person feels guilty for having asked you in the first place: 'How could you even ask me; you know how pressured I am.'

Although these kind of refusals get you off the hook, they can leave you with a hangover of unpleasant feelings. If you believe, for instance, that saying 'no' is always an uncaring or mean act, then you will be left feeling guilty; if you believe that people won't respect you if you refuse them, you will be left feeling resentful. You might decide that these feelings are so painful that it would be better for you to say 'yes'. But this isn't a very satisfactory solution to the problem, because you are in danger of ending up feeling out of control of your life.

> *Exercise: Think about a time you agreed to something that you wish you had refused. Replay the situation in your mind or write down the conversation. How did you communicate your reaction? What was the outcome? How were you left feeling?*

If you are not able and willing to say 'no' with confidence and authority you run the risk of having a great deal of your time stolen. You will, for instance, have to deal with people persisting in their requests because they think they will be able to persuade you. Your self-esteem will suffer because you can be left feeling weak and vulnerable.

When you are being asked for something which you do not want to give, your response should be influenced by the nature of the relationship between you and the other person. The relationship may be important to you and though on this occasion you want to refuse the person, you will not want to make things worse between you. In this case you need to make a thoughtful, careful response along the following lines:

Step 1:   CHECK: The first step is to check that you understand what is being asked of you. You can do this by reflecting back to the person what you understand them to be asking you. Listen carefully to what the person is saying and reflect back to them, in your own words, the content and feelings as you understand them. E.g. 'I just want to check I understand what you want. You would like me to work late tomorrow because you're worried that we won't be able to fill the order in time.'

Step 2:   THINK: Don't answer right away. Take a moment to think whether the request is reasonable or not and whether you want to do it or not. (You may decide a request is reasonable but not want to do it or that it is unreasonable but you are willing to do it). If you need time to think, ask for it. 'I would like time to think about what you've asked. Please give me a minute/five minutes/a day . . .' It's useful to have a checklist of questions you can quickly ask yourself before you make your decision, e.g.:

> How long will this take?
> What is likely to happen if I say 'no'?
> What will I have to drop in order to take this on?
> Have I got the skill/knowledge to do this?
> Am I clear exactly what is involved?
> How will I feel if I say 'yes'?
> How will I feel if I say 'no'?
> What reward is there in this for me?
> What cost will there be?

If you haven't got enough information to make a decision, try saying, 'I don't know. I need some more information.'

Step 3:   DECIDE: Decide whether the answer will be 'yes' or 'no'. Learn to take account of your body's reaction to the requests made of you. Sometimes you will be very clear. You might feel the buzz of excitement or pleasure and want to say 'yes' immediately. Or you may get that sinking feeling which signals reluctance, and you know that you want to say 'no'. It's more difficult when the immediate reaction is less obvious. However, since your body will always have a reaction, get into the habit of listening for it.

I'm not suggesting that you always go with your 'gut' reaction; but you use it as a guide. The danger of ignoring it is that you may agree to something, and then spend ages regretting it and kicking yourself for not realizing that you really should have refused.

'If 'no', you can use this formula:

The 'No' Formula

1 Repeat what it is you have been asked to do: 'You are asking me if . . .'; 'What you want me to do is . . .'

2 Share what you are thinking and feeling about it. 'I feel worried because I don't know how I will fit this in with my work load'; 'I am angry because I haven't been given any notice of the change'; 'I would like to help you but I have already promised to give priority to the work I am now doing'; 'I am afraid that if I say 'No' it will be held against me in some way.'

3 State your decision clearly. 'I have decided to say 'No' on this occasion'; 'I'm afraid I can't take this on'; 'I don't want to do this.'

4 Say why you are refusing: '. . . because I won't be able to meet the other agreements I have made'; '. . . because I don't have the skills to do this'; '. . . because it's not what we agreed' '. . . because I don't think I will enjoy it.'

5 Reflect any response you think the other person is having to your 'No'. 'I realize this isn't what you wanted to hear'; 'I can see that it leaves you with a problem'; 'It looks like you're angry at my response . . .' 'I can see you're disappointed . . .'

6 If you are willing to be asked again, say so: 'I'm sorry I'm not able to help you out this evening, but I'm free later in the week.'

7 If you are willing to negotiate, offer the opportunity: 'However, I'm willing to discuss any suggestions for solving the problem'; 'If you can give me a couple of hours to finish what I am doing now, I'll take the children this afternoon'.

> *Exercise:* Think of a time when you have agreed to something you would rather have refused. Write out, or replay in your mind, what you actually said and did at the time. Then rewrite the scene using the formula:
>
> What you want is ....; I think/feel ....; I have decided ....because ....; However ....
>
> Practise saying your formula out loud. Don't be put off if it sounds stilted to begin with. Repeat it several times until you can say it without referring to what you have written. You will find that with each repetition, it becomes easier and more natural.

This formula is a good approach for handling a refusal so that the other person isn't left feeling rejected or unheard. However, there may be occasions where you don't want to give reasons or engage in any negotiations. You may just want the person to stop making their demands because they are unreasonable or because they won't take 'no' for an answer. In this situation, the well-known assertion technique called 'Broken Record' is very useful.

The Broken Record 'No':   It works by repeating a short sentence over and over again, like a broken record. It is very helpful in getting your message over to someone who is harassing or trying to manipulate you. Here is an example which shows how Henry dealt with the attempts of the host at a party to offer him a drink:

Host: What can I get you to drink? Champagne? Whisky? Wine?

Henry: Thanks for offering. I'm not drinking this evening.

Host: Henry! It's a party. Come on, just one.

Henry: No thanks, I'm not drinking this evening.

Host: Don't be such a party-pooper!

Henry: I'm not drinking this evening.

Host: Look. Everyone else is enjoying themselves. What harm will a small whisky do?

Henry: I realize you're worried that I'm not enjoying myself. I'm having a good time and I'm not drinking this evening.

Host: Okay. I guess you know best what you want.

The goal is to be clear about what you want to say and to make this known without getting angry, uncomfortably irritated or loud. It's useful in situations where you don't want to engage in a dialogue. It can be very effective with doorstep or telephone salespeople. It allows you to be assertive without being rude or aggressive.

The two stages are:

(1) Identify your goal and make a clear statement:

- It's not possible for me to work this evening.'

- 'No, I'm afraid I can't lend you any money.'

- 'I'm not interested in buying double-glazing.'

- 'I'd like my money back please.'

(2) Repeat the message without picking up on any counter statement which will cloud the issue:

  - 'But the point is . . .'
  - 'I don't think you heard me. I can't . . .'
  - 'Maybe I haven't been clear . . .'
  - 'That's really irrelevant to the main issue . . .'
  - 'I realize this is a problem for you, but . . .'

Helpful general points:

- Don't be diverted into discussing past situations.

- 'You're right, I have lent you money in the past but on this occasion I can't lend you any money.'

- Look as if you mean what you say.

- If you are afraid that you will have difficulty staying on track if the other person tries to persuade you – write down in advance what you want to say; practise and memorize it.

- If an important side issue comes up, you can say, 'I'd like to talk about that as soon as we have settled this . . .'

- If the other person does not seem to be hearing or understanding you, try asking them to reflect. 'What do you think I am saying?' or 'What do you understand my position to be at the moment?'

Exercise: Think of a time when you were hassled into agreeing to something when you really wanted to refuse. Work out your Broken Record sentence and practise saying it. Get a friend to

*play the scene with you so that you can get used
to calmly making your point.*

Watch Your Body

However you say 'no', it is important that your body language
gives the same message. Our bodies tend to communicate our
state of mind very accurately. This language is communicated
through small gestures, eye movements, change in posture and
facial expression. Non-verbal messages can either confirm or can-
cel out what you are saying. You may have rehearsed how you are
going to refuse and say all the right things, but your body can
give you away. Your tone of voice, your posture, your facial expression might be telling a different story.

Posture: Practice saying 'no' in front of a mirror. Are
you standing upright or slouching so that your head
drops and your shoulders hunch up. Are you off-
balance, with your weight on one leg? Is your head
upright or cocked to one side? If your posture
communicates anxiety or defensiveness, you are not
likely to be taken seriously. Try standing so that your
weight is equally balanced on your legs, let your back
straighten and your shoulders relax, imagine that a
string is pulling up the top of your head so that your
neck lengthens. Take a couple of slow deep breaths –
and you are ready to face the world.

Something else to consider is your height relative to
that of the other person. For instance, if you are sitting
down and the other person is towering above you,
you're bound to feel at a disadvantage. Stand up so that
you are on a more equal footing.

Eyes: Our eyes are powerful communicators. Just think
what it's like trying to talk to someone who refuses to
look at you. It's also difficult to talk to someone who
insists on staring at you without shifting their gaze.
You need to aim at something in between. Your gaze
needs to be relaxed and friendly. If you don't look
directly at the person to whom you are saying 'no' you

may be perceived as embarrassed, unfriendly or timid. On the other hand, if you glare unblinkingly, you could be seen as hostile or aggressive. It is helpful also to be aware of cultural differences with regard to acceptable and appropriate body language. For instance, in some cultures direct eye contact is taken as a sign of disrespect.

Face: Apart from the eyes, the face itself communicates. A clenched jaw, tightly pressed or trembling lips, frowning forehead, raised eyebrows all send signals and may detract from the message you want the other person to receive. Another powerful influence is your smile. Smiling can mean a lot of different things. At its best, our smile shows that we are feeling safe and happy and enjoying whatever is happening. A smile can be encouraging or comforting. On the other hand, a smile can also signal nervousness or uncertainty. We can use a smile to cover what it is that we would really like to be saying. Smiling tends to diminish the power of the message, so that it is less likely to be taken seriously.

Voice: Tone and volume are as important as the actual words you speak. If you are too soft you might be ignored; if you are too loud you may be perceived as hectoring. If you have access to a tape recorder, make a tape of your voice. Firstly check the volume and speed with which you speak. Can you be heard clearly? Are you speaking very quickly? Notice whether your voice comes over as whiny, apologetic, sarcastic or hostile.

Practise speaking clearly and slowly; breathing and relaxation will help release the throat and chest muscles which constrict under stress. If you tend to speak in a monotone, experiment with the upper and lower registers of your voice.

If your voice reflects confidence and firmness, rather than half-heartedness or hostility, you are much more likely to be listened to and understood.

Gestures: Are you a hair-twiddler, hand-twitcher, foot-tapper, nail-biter? All of these kinds of gestures can be interpreted as messages about your state of mind.

If you are uncertain about the impression you are giving, try to get some feedback from friends or, even better, make a video film of yourself. Once you become aware of the messages you might be communicating through body language, you can learn to have more control over it. Even slight adjustments can make a difference. Standing a little straighter, breathing a little deeper, keeping your hands and feet still, all can make you feel calmer and more in control.

Practice Makes Perfect: Practise saying the word 'no'. It can be surprisingly difficult to get the word out of your lips, especially after a lifetime of believing that you shouldn't really say it at all.

> *Exercise: Stand in front of a mirror. Make a caricature of saying 'no' in the worst possible way. Drop your head, shift from one foot to the other, smile weakly and so on. Now, stand up straight, look yourself in the eye and say 'no' clearly and calmly. Enjoy the feeling of being definite and clear.*

Watch out for excessive apology or excuses. An explanation is not the same thing as an excuse! If you find yourself going into a long explanation, ask yourself for whose benefit this is. You may be using time dealing with your own anxieties rather than giving the other person information they really want or need. If you've ever been at the receiving end of one of those long, apologetic, excuse-ridden refusals you'll know what I mean!

The Guilt Trap

If you're still feeling uncomfortable about all of this, maybe you're caught in the guilt trap into which it is so easy to fall. Many of us have grown up with a strong sense of our obligation to other people. As children we may have got the early message that to be good we should always put other people's needs before our own. So any time we went about meeting our own needs, we felt bad. This process can leave us with the habit of feeling bad whenever we feel we are putting ourselves first. I am not suggesting that you should ignore the needs of others or that you should always put yourself first. Society would be very bleak if everyone did that. There are times when other people should have priority over you. However, what I am suggesting is that you should put yourself in the picture, considering your needs alongside everyone else's. Your decision to say 'Yes' or 'No' is more likely to be based on the needs of the present situation than on your need to assuage your guilt.

If one of the reasons you find it hard to say 'No' is that you know you will feel guilty afterwards, are you clear where these thoughts and feelings come from?

Your Past

For instance they could be more attached to your past history than to the present moment. The habit of feeling guilty can be created by parents: 'If you do that again, Mummy won't love you any more'; 'How could you behave that way; Daddy will be so disappointed'; 'You're making me ill with your naughtiness'. Or by teachers: 'Your parents are really going to be disappointed in you'; 'How can you behave this way after all your parents have done for you?' Religion can induce guilt with messages like: 'You won't go to Heaven if you are selfish'; 'God is always watching you'; 'It is a sin to think of yourself'. When we were children the idea that we could harm someone or lose our parent's affection by attending to our own needs was very powerful. It didn't stop us having needs, but we learnt to feel bad about them. These reactions can still operate when we are adults and prevent us from dealing with situations in a rational way. We may, for instance, feel so hurt and guilty at the prospect of disappointing someone that we make agreements which are unwise and that we regret.

Breaking a Code

We can feel guilty, too, if we break our own particular moral code. It can be worthwhile to take some time to review your ideas of what is right and wrong, particularly if there is a rule which you find yourself constantly breaking. Maybe you lose your temper often and then feel bad because you believe you should be more tolerant and accepting; perhaps you steal and feel guilty because stealing is wrong. The problem is not that your code is wrong but that you keep breaking it. Feeling guilty obviously doesn't work! It's almost as if by feeling guilty you give yourself permission to continue with the behaviour.

Consider the idea that although feeling guilty is not at all pleasant, you may actually be choosing it. Believe it or not, there are rewards for feeling guilty. For instance:

- It is often easier to feel guilty than to do the work necessary actually to change the behaviour that's causing the problem.

- There is a tendency to believe that if you feel guilty enough you will be somehow forgiven for having behaved badly.

- Other people are often impressed by guilt; they mistake it for caring. But guilt is not really caring. If you really cared you would do something about changing your behaviour, rather than talk about how guilty you feel.

- Guilt is a wonderful way of getting sympathy from other people.

- Feeling guilty can have the effect of stopping you from changing and so you don't need to face the risks that inevitably go with change.

- Being able to blame people for making you feel guilty is a good way of not taking responsibility for your own actions.

Eliminating guilt from your life is possible, but only if you are willing to be responsible for taking the necessary action for dismissing it. You need to:

- Realize that the past can never be changed. If you are

feeling guilty about things done or not done in the past, accept that however guilty you feel, you cannot change what happened. Ask yourself, 'Is there anything I can do now to make things better?' and if there is, do it. If there isn't, ask yourself what you should learn and learn it! Then the guilt will have served a constructive purpose and you can let it go.

- Ask yourself whether there is anything you are avoiding in the present by immersing yourself in guilt about the past. Facing the present will release you from the trap of past guilt.

- Decide to accept those things about yourself which you have chosen but which others may dislike. If you become more assertive about saying 'No' it is natural that others will be put out or disappointed. If you are sure that you are making reasonable, clear and thoughtful decisions, the approval of other people will not be so important to you.

- Re-evaluate your personal code of conduct. Which values do you really believe in and which do you only pay lip-service to? Create a value system in which you can believe and to which you are willing to subscribe.

- If there are people in your life who are able to manipulate you with guilt, let them know clearly that you are willing and able to take responsibility for your own actions and decisions. So the next time, for instance, that someone says, 'You will make sure my clothes are ironed in time for me to go out tonight, won't you', you will reply with 'I haven't planned to do any ironing today. I'm willing to get the ironing board out for you to use if you like.'

Exercise: Make a list of all the bad things you can remember doing. Rate them on a scale one to ten. Now add up your score. Take time to feel guilty about each one and give each item another rating

*related to the amount of guilt you feel about it.
Now see what difference all that has made.
Nothing will have changed – the past is the past
and the present moment is still the same.*

*If you want to continue with this exercise, ask
yourself what you could learn from each item and
what you will decide as a result of the learning.
Write this down and then say to yourself, 'I release
myself from feeling guilty about . . . because I
have learned . . . and as a result have decided . . .'
Repeat this each time you begin to feel guilty.*

Another Trap?

Having explored the guilt trap, let's take a look at the worry trap.
Whereas guilt is usually about the past, worry is more often
about the future. For instance, we may not permit ourselves to
say 'No' to someone because of worry about how they might be
affected.

Just as feeling guilty in itself does not solve or change anything, so it is with worry. You can spend a lot of time worrying
but not one moment will make things any easier. One reason is
that much of our worry is about things we can't control. You cannot foresee the future and you have no control over how people
will react to you.

Guilt and worry are self-defeating patterns of thinking and
feeling. If you get caught in them, your behaviour is more likely
to be controlled by the people whom you want to protect or please.
There are times in your life when it is healthy, appropriate and
wise for you to say 'No' to people. Don't let guilt or worry trap you
into allowing others to control how you use the time of your life.

*Exercise: Just as you identified the things you felt
guilty about, now list those things which cause you
worry. There will be small personal matters and
more global worries about the nature of the world.
When you have done this, sit back and worry as
hard as you can for at least five minutes.*

Often people laugh when I suggest this exercise. They suddenly see the ridiculous side of using time in this way. When the five minutes is up, ask yourself, 'What has changed as a result of my worrying?' The answer is always 'Nothing' (well, except that some people do feel a bit more depressed or powerless). Consider each item on your list and just as you did with your guilt list, decide whether you can DO anything about them. Where you can, do it. Where you can't, let it go from your mind to clear space for more productive thoughts.

The Other Side of Saying 'No'

We have concentrated on how to get your needs met by being clear about when you want to say 'No'. You can also get your needs met by asking for what you want. For some people this is just as difficult as saying 'No'. Stating the wish and making a direct request seems too simple and direct. Sometimes we may resort to hinting and hoping the other person can read our mind; sometimes we decide to do without altogether. Why is it so difficult?

Maybe your fear is being refused and as a result feeling hurt or rejected. This doesn't really make sense if you think about it. You haven't got something at the moment; you ask for it from someone; they don't give it to you; you haven't got it. But you never had it in the first place – so what have you actually lost? You do have a right to ask anything from anybody – you don't, of course, have a right to get it! The other person's right is to decide whether to give you all, some or nothing. However, if you don't ask in the first place you can't really blame the other person for denying you.

Perhaps you are afraid that asking for something will leave you feeling exposed and vulnerable. Maybe the fear is about losing face or destroying your image as the person who can cope with everything. Again this needs thinking through. In a way, this response shows a basic mistrust of others; as if people who knew your deepest needs would use the knowledge against you in some way. There is some truth to this perception because there are indeed some people who bolster their own inadequacies by manipulating others. However, in intimate relationships, saying what you want is more sensible and effective. A good relationship will be strengthened by this kind of honest direct communication.

One of the ways in which some people solve this problem for themselves is not to ask for anything unless they are pretty certain their requests will be granted. In this way they can't 'lose face' or suffer the hurt of rejection. On the other hand, this can easily become a power game. Take the executive, for instance, who surrounds him or herself with 'yes-people'.

In a healthy relationship, each person is free to ask for what he or she wants from the other; the other is free to say 'Yes' or 'No' according to his or her wants. The relationship continues whether the request is granted or not with no hard feelings from either party.

It is important, though, to understand the difference between a request and a demand. To make a genuine request you say where you are and what you would like from the other person in such a way that they feel free to accept or refuse.

A request becomes a demand if you let the other person know that you expect or are entitled to a certain answer, or that you will feel hurt, rejected, angry or abandoned if you are denied.

Are you familiar with this kind of thing? 'Mum, can I stay out all night at the party? Everyone else's parents are letting them stay late.' (*Translation: If you don't let me do what I want you're mean and not as good as everyone else's mother.*) 'Angie, can you call in at the Post Office and get some stamps and collect my dry cleaning on your way home? You've got to go out anyway and I took your shoes in to be repaired last week.' (*You've got to do what I say because you owe me.*)

This kind of emotional manipulation is not acceptable if you are aiming for honest communication. Moreover a great deal of time is frittered away as a result of not communicating your wants and needs directly. So get into the habit of refusing what you don't want and asking for what you do want.

In this chapter we have explored how a reluctance to say 'No' steals time away. Next we are going to look at how to spend time looking after yourself in order to save time for the changes you want to make.

7

SPEND TIME TO SAVE TIME

At the beginning of the book we considered the way that stress affects our thoughts, feelings and behaviour. This chapter shows how to devise a self-care programme to help you use your time to the best possible advantage. Learning to manage stress will take time but it will be time well spent. It is just like learning any other mental or physical skill that takes time and effort to master. With daily use, your programme will soon become a habit and you will notice the benefits. Set aside a time each day to practise whichever of the exercises you select and they will soon become second nature to you.

Don't be put off by thinking that these are things that are too difficult to learn. Or that the whole process will be too boring and tedious. Do you remember how you learnt to read? Perhaps you were one of those lucky people who seemed to have a natural talent and learned with almost no effort. Maybe you painfully learned the alphabet by repeating it over and over again; then you learned how to put the letters together to make words. You started with something like: 'The cat sat on the mat,' and worked your way up to your present level. However hard you had to work at it, you managed it. It is the same with any skill. The work involved can seem dull and boring, but it does not have to be. It is possible to make any learning interesting – remember the colours and pictures in your early reading books? You probably remember those teachers when you were at school who were able to fire your imagination with creative lessons. In the same way you can use your imagination to develop your own learning plan.

Each section of this chapter will introduce a technique for reducing the symptoms of stress. They are all tried and tested although it is likely that some will appeal to you more than others. Select the ones that you find attractive and start with those if you wish. You might, though, find it worthwhile to experiment with the ones you don't immediately like or understand. You may find a technique that works very well for you and add it to your repertoire. Re-reading the chapter on goal setting as you devise your own personal self-care programme is also a good idea! It will help you to make sure that you are not actually increasing your stress level.

The Refreshment of Relaxation

Has anyone ever told you to relax just when you know it's the last thing you can do? Sitting in the dentist's chair for instance. Or just before an important test? Even in situations like these you can learn to relax. Learning how to relax is one of the best ways of helping yourself to manage stress and is usually included in stress management programmes. But like any skill, it does have to be learnt.

The reason it is so important is that unnecessary muscle tension wastes energy. As we have seen in Chapter 1, the fight or flight response, which helps you respond quickly to physical threat, can do more harm than good if it is triggered too frequently and the effects are not fully discharged. The nervous system has a two-part response, the sympathetic and the parasympathetic. When the fight or flight response is triggered, it is the sympathetic system which goes into action. This increases your arousal level and sets in train the series of reactions which produces more energy for you to deal with the threat.

On the other hand, the parasympathetic system reduces the level of arousal and calms you down. When activated, it reverses the effects of the sympathetic reaction. For instance, breathing and heart rate return to previous levels; the circulation redistributes blood back to the digestive system so that digestion can proceed; blood pressure drops; the cooling system returns to normal. It is the parasympathetic side of the autonomic nervous system which balances the intense activity of the sympathetic side. When one is in operation the other lies dormant. One of the things that happens if we spend too much time under pressure is that we can lose the ability to activate the parasympathetic response which would have a calming effect on our body.

When the threat that has triggered the fight/flight response has passed it takes some time for the level of arousal to decrease. It is possible that long before the process is complete, another threat has arisen and the sympathetic system comes into play again. So our bodies never really get the chance to discharge the energy and get back to normal. It is easy to see how the wear and tear which this constant state of physical and mental activation creates ends up in one or other of the well-known stress illnesses. You reach a point where you feel too tired to relax!

Learning relaxation techniques is one way to take control of the balance of your reaction to stress. Relaxation is more than just flopping into a chair at the end of a long, hard day or calling in at the pub for a drink to unwind.

> *Exercise: Sit in a comfortable upright position and tense all your muscles as much as you can. Hold them tense for a few seconds and then let them go. What do you notice? One thing that probably happened is that when you let the tension go you also breathed out. While your muscles were tense, you were also holding your breath.*

Breathing and an awareness of muscle tension are the two main elements of relaxation.

Let's consider breathing first. As tension rises, triggering the sympathetic system, you breathe faster and more shallowly. To bring the parasympathetic system into play you need to breathe more slowly and deeply. Concentrate on breathing out rather than breathing in. The temptation under stress is to breathe in and then hold the breath. Think back to the exercise you have just done. Focusing on breathing out is an effective way of triggering the calming parasympathetic system.

The next consideration is the tension in your muscles. If you have become accustomed to living at a high level of arousal you may not notice the tension in your muscles unless they become too painful to be ignored. Easing the tension out of the muscles is important. One easy way to do this is to stretch just like a cat so that the muscles tense and then relax.

Developing and using the skill of relaxation will take some

time. But regular relaxation will improve your ability to deal with pressure. It will restore the balance in your nervous system as well as alleviating some of the effects of stress. You are likely to sleep better and your digestive system will benefit.

Here is an exercise which takes one relaxation technique in stages. Since to be really effective you need to close your eyes, it is a good idea to read through all the stages before you start. You could record it on a tape so that you can play it through each time you practise. Another idea is to do this together with a friend and take it in turns to take one another through the process. This particular relaxation technique is based on consciously tightening and then relaxing muscle groups. Don't overstrain the muscles as you tense them. Tighten them firmly – but not so hard that they quiver with the effort. If you are worried about physical problems that might be affected by this kind of exercise, check with your GP before you start.

The temperature of the room should be comfortably warm. If it is too cold or if your muscles are very tired, you might get mild cramp. If that happens gently kneading the affected muscles will usually relieve the tension.

You might find you have trouble keeping awake and if this is the case practise in the sitting, rather than lying, position. The point of these relaxation exercises is to learn to relax when you are awake! Falling asleep rather defeats the object. If you find you constantly nod off while you do the exercises, it is probably a sign that you need to do something about the amount of sleep you are getting. You might find it useful to hold an unbreakable object loosely in one hand; if you begin to nod off, it will fall to the floor and wake you up.

Exercise:

    1: Find a comfortable position in a chair, on a bed or on the floor. Lying down is better because not so many of your muscles will be involved in maintaining the sitting position. You can make yourself more comfortable lying down by placing small cushions under your head and knees. Close your eyes.

119

2: *Take a moment to get a sense of how you are at the moment without doing anything about it. Notice how your body feels and the things you are thinking about.*

3: *Focus on your breathing by putting one hand just below your rib cage. Breathe in through your nose, taking air to the bottom of your lungs so that your hand is pushed outwards. Fill your lungs right to the bottom, letting them expand. Hold this for a few seconds. Now slowly breathe out through your mouth. When you reach the end of the breath, blow out just a little more so that you really empty your lungs. Repeat this a few times until you find a comfortable rhythm.*

4: *Now focus on your muscles. If you are sitting, put your hands in your lap; if you are lying, place them by your sides.*

First concentrate on your feet. Tighten the muscles in your feet as hard as you can and hold them tense for a few seconds. Now let go. Tighten them again . . . and let go.

Now concentrate on your lower legs. Tighten your calf muscles, hold the tension for a few seconds and then let go. Tighten again . . . and let go.

Now concentrate on your thigh muscles. Tighten them, hold the tension for a few seconds and then let go. Tighten again . . . and let go.

Now move your awareness to your buttocks. Tighten the muscles, hold the tension for a few seconds and then let go. Tighten again . . . and let go.

Now move your awareness to your stomach. Tighten the muscles, pulling them in as much as you can. Hold for a few seconds and then let go. Tighten again . . . and then let go.

Now your back. Arch your back up (or for-ward if you are sitting) as if you had a pillow under the middle and low part of your back and hold for a few seconds. Tighten again . . . and let go.

Now your chest and lungs! Take a deep breath and tighten your chest muscles and hold for a moment. Tighten again . . . and let go.

Now your hands. Clench your fists into a tight ball and hold for a few seconds, then let go. Tighten again . . . then let go.

Now your arms. Tighten the muscles, hold for a few seconds then let go. Tighten again, then let go.

Now your shoulders. Hunch them right up to your ears and hold the tension for a few seconds. Then let them drop. Tighten again . . . then let go.

Now focus on your jaw. Clench your teeth and jaw as hard as you can. Hold for a few seconds then let go. Tighten again . . . then let go.

Now focus on your face. Screw up your eyes tightly and frown as hard as you can, hold for a few seconds. Now let go. Tighten again . . . then let go.

Now take your attention again through your body. If you feel any tension left, ease it out by tightening and letting go that particular group of muscles.

Stay as you are for a while and focus again on your breathing

5: Open your eyes and slowly sit up. Stay sitting

for a moment or two keeping your breathing deep and easy. Now you are ready to face the world.

Plan regular short sessions of relaxation, whenever and wherever suits you. Fifteen or twenty minutes at the same time each day, preferably at least an hour after eating. You need a place that is quiet and where you will be uninterrupted. If you can't find this at work or home, try a quiet park, library or any place where you could be left in peace for half an hour or so. It is important that you schedule a regular place and time for this so that you can keep up the practice.

Get into the habit of checking your body often for signs of tension. When you're held up in a traffic jam, for instance, ask yourself, 'Is my jaw clenched? Are my shoulders hunched? Are my hands tight?' Your awareness may be enough for you to relax consciously and in time this will be second nature to you.

Counting Relaxation Counting down from ten to zero for relaxation is also a very effective technique. The brief time needed to count backwards can break the spiral of anxiety and tension. If you notice you are getting tired, a few seconds in this type of relaxation can be refreshing. The simplest way to do this is to focus on your breathing while counting. Each time you breathe out, say the next number.

Here is a script for a counting relaxation which you can tape for practice.

Count backwards from ten to zero. Silently say each number as you breathe out. As you count you will feel more and more relaxed. When you reach zero you will be completely relaxed.

Ten ... feel the tension drain away; nine ... relax more deeply; eight ... more and more relaxed; seven ... deeper and deeper; six ... let yourself feel calm and relaxed; five ... as the tension drains away your body feels limp and heavy; four ... more and more relaxed; three ... deeper and deeper; two ... very relaxed now;

one . . . you're feeling calm and in control; zero . . . absolutely relaxed.

Keep breathing slowly and deeply and let yourself drift into a feeling of calm and safety. Try to contact a feeling of inner peace, and be aware of this feeling so that you can bring it to mind when you choose.

Now count from one to three; say each number to yourself and take a deep breath with each one. One . . . relaxed but more alert; two . . . still relaxed but wide awake; three . . . eyes open, feeling refreshed. Keep the feeling of relaxation and calm with you as you move into whatever activity you need to do.

Movies in the Mind

You are probably familiar with the way thoughts and images can be upsetting and add to feelings of anxiety and stress. Perhaps you are troubled by what is happening in an important relationship; maybe a particular task at work is not going very well. Thoughts about the problems keep going round and round in your mind, one thought leading to another until you feel at your wits' end. You probably imagine all sorts of disasters occurring as you see yourself trying to improve things. However, you can use your imagination to affect your physical and emotional state positively. Visualization is often used together with relaxation as a powerful technique for calming down or preparing for action.

The basic technique is to form a clear image of a pleasant scene connecting with each of the five senses: e.g. sight – 'see the sparkle of the sun on the water'; smell – 'smell the scent of the flowers'; taste – 'taste the salt from the sea on your lips'; touch – 'feel the smoothness of the rock-face'; sound – 'hear the waves breaking on the shore.'

Start with basic relaxation and breathing and create the pictures in your mind. Here is a sample script:

Start by getting as comfortable as you can. Close your eyes and take a deep breath. Breathe out slowly and easily. Repeat this until you find a comfortable rhythm.

Picture yourself walking along the side of a lake. The sun is shining and there is a pleasant wind blowing.

The water is clear and sparkling. You can hear birdsong and smell the clean pine of a nearby forest. The water is barely lapping along the shore of the lake. You see a small boat tied up. You step into it and find some cushions in the bottom. You lie on the cushions and untie the boat. Now you are floating along, the boat is rocking gently from the motion of the water. As the boat carries you along you can feel the warm sunlight. You are relaxed, peaceful and calm. The gentle rocking motion induces feelings of peace and you become more and more relaxed.

You drift deeper and deeper into your feelings of relaxation. As you continue to float along you are aware of the gentle breeze, the lapping water and the birds and animals on the shore. You are lazily drifting deeper and deeper into a profound feeling of peace until the boat washes up against the shore. You remain, for a moment, in the still boat feeling totally relaxed.

You can use the power of your mind to create a feeling of relaxation whenever you want. If during the rest of the day you find yourself getting upset, remember the feelings of relaxation you have just experienced. Take a deep breath and as you breathe out, see yourself in the boat on the lake and let yourself recreate the pleasant, peaceful feelings.

Now count from one to three. Take a deep breath as you say each number. When you reach three, open your eyes. You will feel relaxed and alert, back in the place where you started the exericse.

Make your own personal movie; conjure up a picture of a place that you find pleasant such as:

Lying on a beach
Walking through a valley
Sitting beside a stream
Climbing to a mountain top
Floating on a cloud
Being on a desert island ...

You can buy tapes of recorded relaxation exercises. If you are guiding yourself, read the instructions a few times before you start. You can ask someone to read the script slowly to you or you can record it yourself and then use the tape to practise. If you record a tape yourself remember to speak slowly with pauses.

Meditation

Meditation is the discipline of relaxing your mind in order to focus your energy. There isn't really a 'right' way to meditate; there are many approaches and you may need to try several before you find a system that suits you. Here is an example:

> *Find a place in which you can sit comfortably and without interruptions. There is no need to sit in a special position. Just make sure you are well supported and comfortable.*
> *Breathe slowly and deeply and create an image in your mind of an object which has some meaning for you. A candle, a star, a vase for example. Hold this image in your mind. You will find that at first your mind wanders and you start thinking of other things. When that happens, gently bring your mind back to the image.*

You may want to set a timer so that you don't have to worry about when to finish. Fifteen to twenty minutes is a reasonable period to start with. As with the relaxation and breathing exercises, make a regular time and place so that you get into the habit.

If you find it difficult to work with images, try using a particular word or phrase; e.g. 'Peace'; 'Calm'; 'I am becoming relaxed' which you repeat in your mind. Counting breaths also works well. If you don't want to work with your imagination, you can set up an actual object which you sit in front of and focus on for the designated time.

Exhilarating Exercise

If all this seems too slow and passive for you, perhaps exercise is a better bet. A regular programme of exercise is one of the most useful ways of getting fitter and coping with pressure. It is another example of spending time to save time in the long run.

How you set up a programme depends on your preferences and your present level of health and fitness. If you are well-disciplined you can start a programme of early morning running or an exercise programme which you carry out every day. If you know you are easily distracted, it might well be worth joining the kind of gym where there are instructors who will work with you to create the most effective programme. Regular swimming, too, is very beneficial.

If you like company, you could investigate the many aerobic, dance, keep fit and movement groups which exist in every part of the country. Tennis, squash, golf, bowls, cricket and football are all games which provide the pleasure of friendly competition and valuable exercise.

If you are thinking of starting up an exercise programme, it is wise to check with your general practitioner first. Whether you choose to exercise on your own or with others; play sports or join groups, regularity is important if you want to get the best benefit from your efforts. A generally recommended frequency is at least three times a week, scheduled throughout the week.

Even if you don't feel like starting a regular programme, there are several ways in which you can become more active and give your body healthy exercise. For instance:

- Walking upstairs instead of relying on lifts and elevators. Start by walking up just one flight and increase at your own pace.

- Deliberately take the long way round rather than a short cut.

- Get off the train or bus one stop before your actual stop and walk the rest of the way.

- If you have a dog, take it for a longer walk than usual.

- If you are using the car for small journeys, walk instead.

- If you take coffee or lunch breaks during the day, go for a walk, or a swim if there is a convenient pool nearby.

One very important benefit of exercise is muscle relaxation. We have seen how, in response to stress, our bodies often become tense. After exercise, the muscles are left relaxed and calm. Exercise can also clear the mind. Very often, if you have a problem which is proving difficult to solve, going for a walk, run or swim gives valuable time for the mind to sort things out.

Time to Indulge

Relaxation and exercise are important parts of any self-care programme and if they become regular activities, the time you spend on them will provide you with a good return. Time spent pampering yourself can also be well spent. You may have got into the frame of mind that time is too precious to spend any of it on pure self-indulgence. However, the theme of this chapter is that looking after yourself will save you time because your body will be fitter and stronger and your mind clearer as a result.

But we are more than just a mind and body machine. We have a spirit and feelings which also need attention. Anyone who has ever been depressed will know how the state of our spirit can lift us or bring us down, even when we are in good physical and mental shape. The intention behind the following suggestions is to encourage you to spend time attending to your feelings as an important contribution to your overall health.

Strokes for Folks: Massage is one of the oldest therapies around and is a wonderful way to escape the tyranny of time. If you can afford it, having massage as a regular part of your self-care programme will pay dividends. It is often discounted by busy people as merely a beauty treatment or a cure for sports injuries, but it is much more than that. Massage can provide a means to counteract the relentless pressures of a busy lifestyle. In its most simple form it is a curative treatment for the muscles and the body's soft tissue. Stroking, rubbing and kneading the body helps to relieve tension and increase the flexibility of tight muscles. Massage techniques also improve blood and lymph circulation to ensure that oxygen and nutrients are carried to cells, tissue and the internal organs. Waste products which get trapped in tight muscles are broken down so that the body can eliminate them. Massage is acknowledged as an antidote to stress. The aim of a professional massage practitioner is to work with the body's ability to heal itself. There are a range of different approaches.

Massage involves systematically stroking, kneading and pressing the soft tissues of the entire body; Shiatsu is a Japanese system which is given with fingers, thumbs, elbows, knees or feet. Whereas massage works mainly on the muscles, ligaments and tendons and affects the body's balance of blood and lymph, Shiatsu concentrates on pressure points in order to affect the balance of energy in the body. Reflexology is based on the theory that there are reflex areas in the feet which are connected to different parts of the body. The practitioner works over the foot as a way of affecting the whole body. Aromatherapy is a form of massage in which essential oils are selected to suit the personality and condition of the person.

If your finances won't stretch to regular massage by an expert, why not get together with a friend and teach yourselves from one of the very good manuals which have been published. *The Book of Massage* by Lucinda Lidell, with Sara Thomas, Carola Beresford Cooke and Anthony Porter (Ebury Press, 1990) is a good example. Touch is of vital importance to us as human beings; it gives us reassurance and comfort and lets us know we are not alone. It is a language we all use instinctively to show our feelings. When we want to show sympathy or reassurance we touch, hold or stroke someone. You don't need to be an expert to learn a simple massage sequence.

If there isn't anyone around that you want to ask, then you can go it alone. You can reach most of your body yourself and providing you take your time and don't hurt yourself by straining to reach areas like the middle of your back, you can give yourself a good massage.

A self-massage sequence: You will need oil or cream. Any oil will do – the best is sweet almond or grapeseed. Start by kneading the sole of one foot and extend this to include the whole foot. Pay some attention to each toe, and then focus on the ankle. Relax for a few minutes and then work on the other foot. Relax for a brief time and then work on your calves. Use long strokes, putting the pressure on the upward stroke. Knead the muscles at

*the back of your leg. Then concentrate on your knees,
rubbing them with circular strokes. Focus then on your
thigh muscles, and work up your stomach and chest,
rubbing in the oil or cream gently and firmly. Work
down your arms and spend some time massaging each
hand. Work on the joints and finish by gently pulling
each finger. Massage the parts of your back that you can
reach, particularly along the top of your shoulders where
a great deal of tension collects. You can also reach the
bottom of your spine and using both hands massage the
muscles at each side of the vertebrae as far as you can.
Finish by giving yourself a face massage, and rubbing
your scalp with the tips of your fingers as if you were
shampooing your hair.*

Take a Bath A long, relaxing bath is an ideal way to indulge
yourself. You don't need anyone else and there are a great range
of oils, herbs or lotions you can add to make it even more pleasant.

Foot baths are particularly soothing; sitting with your feet in a
bowl of warm water, perhaps with oil added, quietly relaxing or
meditating for five or ten minutes is a great way to feel good all
over.

Get Away From It All Another possibility is that you take
some time away from your everyday pressure. If you can afford it
you could consider a day or two at a health farm. These centres
usually offer comfortable accommodation, three healthy meals a
day and a range of treatments such as sauna, steam baths, massage and so on. A stay can be a marvellous fillip to the spirits.
They tend to be expensive, though. Other ways of getting away
include taking a holiday for a change of scene; staying in a retreat
centre where you can have long periods of quiet meditation or, as
a cheaper alternative, exchanging houses with a friend who lives
in a very different environment for a short period of time.

Food for Thought No chapter on self-care would be complete
without a mention of food and there are many theories about

what is and what isn't healthy eating. There do seem to be certain things upon which most experts agree and so you should probably consider them. One of the ways of managing stress is to find ways of reducing the immediate pressure and get some short-term comfort and satisfaction. Most of these do little harm in moderation, problems only arise if they become habits which you turn to whether you are under pressure or not. Examples of these 'props' are cigarettes, tranquillizers, alcohol, coffee, junk food and sweets.

Smoking For many people smoking is a way of relaxing or getting strength to deal with a particularly stressful situation. Several needs can be met by tobacco. The rituals of offering and lighting cigarettes can help get over awkward social situations; the pleasure of inhaling and exhaling the smoke can give a feeling of immediate satisfaction. These satisfactions can all seem at the time more compelling than the knowledge that smoking is harmful to your health. And although it appears that smoking helps deal with stress, in fact it does not. The physiological effects of smoking create more stress for your body to deal with. Breathing and relaxation exercises are more effective ways of reducing stress in the long term – but they don't provide the immediate short-term satisfactions. If you are a smoker, think about what you are actually getting from it – and whether the costs are worth the benefits.

Tranquillizing drugs Doctors sometimes prescribe tranquillizers or sleeping pills to help you deal with stress and they can be very effective. Again the problem is connected to potential long-term problems. It is easy to become dependent on them and some lose their potency if you take them for a long time. If you have become dependent, you may suffer unpleasant withdrawal symptoms when you stop taking them.

Alcohol Alcohol abuse is now seen as a serious problem. In moderation alcohol can add to the pleasure of a meal or a social occasion. But alcohol does have an effect on certain parts of the brain. One of the reasons you can feel so good as a result of drinking is that the alcohol can inhibit your ability to make judgements and distort your sense of priorities. As a result you may stop feeling responsible for the things you are actually responsible for. Heavy drinking creates more stress for your body and mind.

Caffeine Coffee, is a prime source of caffeine, which acts as a stimulant increasing the rate at which your heart beats. Once again in moderation this does not cause us a problem, but continuous coffee drinking will produce long-term effects like the disruption of your sleep pattern. Tea and cola also contain caffeine and so are not good alternatives.

Junk food and sweets A diet high in junk food is likely to contain too much sugar, too much fat, too much salt. There is general agreement among dieticians that too much of these three substances is the cause of many serious stress illnesses. There is no diet which will suit everyone.

The most sensible thing is for you to choose a diet which follows general healthy guidelines and which suits you. But don't follow it slavishly so that it becomes a punishment. The occasional bar of chocolate or slice of white bread will not do you any harm.

The word which best sums up what is important with regard to what you eat and drink is balance. Unless you have a particular condition for which a diet is prescribed, aim for a balance of protein, carbohydrate, fats, vitamins and so on.

How Safe is Your Safety Net?

There are times when living your life seems just like walking a tightrope. Keeping your balance with confidence is easier if you know you have a reliable safety net. This means creating a network of safety zones to which you can retreat when you are hurt, confused or tired.

Exercise: This is a chance to think about the nature of the safety net you have created for yourself.

VALUES: Other exercises have suggested that you examine your belief system and dispose of or change any beliefs which are not appropriate. It is important that you have a set of values which can guide you when you are confused or uncertain.

PLACES: Where can you go when you feel the need for contact with roots and security?

GROUPS: Do you belong to any groups or organizations which give you a sense of belonging and support?

ACTIVITIES: What hobbies, activities or interests can you turn to for recreation and pleasure?

If this exercise has left you with any indication that there are some holes in your safety net, now is the time to begin mending them.

Last, but not least, PEOPLE: Having people to whom you can turn when you need support, help or comfort is very important. Most of us have a range of needs, so it is useful to develop a network of people so that you are not depending on just one or two people. The following exercise will help you identify just who is in your own network.

Exercise: Write in the names of people who fulfil the various types of support for you:

_____ *is someone I can always rely on to listen to me without judging me unfairly.*

_____ *is someone I enjoy chatting to.*

_____ *always makes me feel competent and valued.*

132

_____ gives me truthful and constructive feedback.

_____ is a source of useful and reliable information.

_____ is constantly introducing me to new ideas and new people.

_____ challenges and encourages me to think about what I am doing.

_____ is dependable in a crisis.

_____ is someone to whom I feel emotionally close.

_____ is someone with whom I can share negative feelings.

_____ is someone with whom I can share good news and feelings.

Does anything surprise you when you look over the results of this exercise? Have you identified any holes in your safety net? What are the consequences of this for you and other people? If you want to make any changes, what are they? Will they be reliable and serve you well in future?

The Last Word

It is important to guard against allowing any of the techniques discussed in this chapter to become new tyrants in your life. You could make a martyr of yourself by slavishly following an exercise routine you hate or doing relaxation exercises in every spare minute. If you make a chore of any of the things you decide to try you will probably only keep it up for a week or two but then go back to old habits. Choose items which suit you and which you will enjoy.

It won't be easy to make the decision to give time to look after yourself if you have values and beliefs which tell you it is wrong to do so.

This quiz will give you a clue as to how easy you might find it to be successful. Read through the statements and mark whether you agree or disagree with each one.

1 I enjoy spending time looking after myself.

2 I feel better when I'm spending time on others rather than myself.

3 I deserve to give attention to myself.

4 Other people matter more than I do.

5 I am assertive in asking for what I need.

6 It would be selfish if I asked for what I wanted.

7 Everyone needs looking after, however old they are.

8 I am not worth spending time on.

9 I will have to fight for any care and attention that I want.

10 Once you are an adult, you shouldn't need looking after.

11 Looking after myself means that I will be better at looking after others.

12 If people really cared about me, they'd meet my needs without my having to ask for anything.

13 Taking responsibility for identifying and looking after my own needs is important.

14 My needs are less important than other people's.

15 I think that putting aside some time to look after myself should take precedence over other activities.

16 I would only spend time looking after myself if I had no other demands on my time.

Score a point each time you agreed with an odd number and disagreed with an even one.

The maximum score is 16. If you scored between 12 and 16 your particular set of beliefs will help you take care of yourself. In fact, you probably already have a very effective self-care programme.

If your score is between 8 and 12 you realize the importance of looking after yourself but you probably feel guilty whenever you do spend time on your own needs.

If you scored between 4 and 8 you have some views which could get in the way of your care of yourself. It would be worth spending time re-evaluating these before you start making plans for your self-care strategy.

If you scored less than 4 you probably find it hard to plan a programme for looking after yourself. You probably haven't enjoyed reading this chapter at all – but don't dismiss it out of hand. Take your time to think about the beliefs you hold and how they might be preventing you from taking good care of yourself.

Taking time to look after yourself has been the theme of this chapter. This will be time well spent; by improving your health and your state of mind you will have put yourself in a much better position to undertake and succeed in your goals. The next chapter reveals one of the biggest thieves of time – procrastination.

8

DON'T DELAY

Procrastination is one of the greatest thieves of time. It works like this: there is something you know you want to do which will bring about some change for you or the people around you. Change always involves some risk because you cannot possibly accurately predict the outcome. Dreaming about it and resolving to do something in the future feels like actually doing it. Thinking about the changes becomes a substitute for action. It feels much safer because no actual risk is taken. The thinking process is something like this: 'I know I want to do this. I'm afraid that I won't do it well enough or that when I've done it I won't like the result. So I'll keep thinking about it until I'm sure about it. As long as I'm thinking about doing this, it remains a possibility. I will do it one day.' This is convenient thinking because it keeps the idea alive but you don't take any risk. However the longer it goes on, the emptier it becomes. There will come a time when you no longer have the choice – for some reason it will be too late. Then your thinking will turn into regret.

Are you:

- Staying in a job which is unfulfilling and in which you feel stuck and unable to progress?

- In the grip of an addiction such as drinking, drugs, smoking; worrying about its effects but not getting down to breaking it?

- Avoiding a confrontation with a particular person, even

136

though bringing what's happening into the open may improve the relationship?

- Putting off mundane tasks like cleaning, repairing, decorating and so on until they build up so much that you just have to do them?

- Living in a place which you don't really like but continue to stay in?

- Deciding to start your diet/exercise/study/practice programme tomorrow?

- Dreaming about the ideal holiday/job/house/partner without doing anything practical to turn the dream into reality?

- Criticising others instead of doing something yourself?

- Saying 'I don't have to do it now'/'I am going to start that right away'/'I'm determined to start tomorrow'/'I'll get round to that later' or similar phrases?

A Vicious Circle

Procrastination can bring feelings of guilt or anxiety. We are caught in a vicious circle – we know we should do something – we put it off so we feel guilty – we think about the effect of not doing it so we feel anxious – so we know we should do it – and so on. There is a certain belief system which supports this behaviour. It is based on such myths as:

- If you leave things alone they will work themselves out.

- If you wish for something hard enough, it will happen.

Words like *hoping, wishing, maybe*, perhaps give you a let-out from taking action. Hoping and wishing are hangovers from the days when we listened to and believed the fairy tales of our childhood. In them, the hero only had to wish for something and it happened; the heroine just waited and her wishes were granted; the fairy godmother waved a wand and changes came about. It would be wonderful if that was how real life operated – but it doesn't. As a general rule, things don't happen unless you make them happen, and while you continue to hope or wish for something you are not likely to do anything. Imagine, for instance, that you are in hospital waiting for a serious operation. You have been prepared for theatre and are just giving into to the pre-med. As you float into unconsciousness, the surgeon walks by your bed and you hear her say 'I hope I get this one right!' How confident would you feel?

It is too glib to say you can do anything you set your mind to. Of course you are dependent on the resources, both internal and external, that you need to carry out your plans. You may not be able to achieve your heart's desires – but you could at least have the satisfaction of knowing that you did your best. It is likely that you are stronger than you think. If you don't test yourself, you will never know what you are actually capable of accomplishing.

> *Exercise: This is a good exercise to do with someone else so that you can share your reactions with each other. Take it in turns to complete the following sentence: 'I am trying to . . .'; repeat it for everything you are trying to do at the moment. When your list has run out, repeat the sentences but this time start 'I intend to . . .'*
>
> *You can repeat this exercise by changing 'I must . . .' into 'I choose to . . .'; 'I can't . . . into 'I won't . . .'; 'I hope . . . into 'I will . . .'*
>
> *Notice how by using words like hope, must, can't and so on you let yourself off the hook of taking responsibility for your actions.*

Rage Spread Thin

Boredom is a spin-off of procrastination. I once heard boredom described as 'rage spread thin' and I think there is a lot of truth in this idea. We feel bored because we have needs which are not being met at the time but our energy feels so thin that we can't or won't do something to change what is happening. One way of looking at the concept of boredom is that it is a choice, something we do to ourselves. Even in the most tedious situations, we have the choice of using our mind creatively. On the other hand, it may be easier to blame our boredom on a person or the environment. 'These people are so dull'; 'This job is monotonous.'

> *Exercise: Think about the last time you were bored. What were the needs that were not being met for you? What was the effect of the boredom?*

Delay Benefits

We have already seen how our behaviour rewards us – even if the behaviour is something with which we are not particularly happy. Here are some of the benefits from hanging on to our delaying tactics:

- Simply, putting something off provides escape from unpleasant activities. If there is something you are afraid to do, for instance, delaying means you don't have to face it.

- The point has already been made that procrastination often brings boredom with it. Being bored means we can blame someone or something else for what's happening. We can think about how bored we are rather than turn our mind to how to bring about the changes we want.

- You will never have to face the risk of failure by avoiding all activities which involve some risk.

- You will never have to face the risks that may go with success. For instance, succeeding raises other people's expectations of you and your own. Success brings responsibilities which you would rather avoid.

- Sympathy is very often forthcoming from other people. Since most of us procrastinate to some extent or other, a lot of strokes get exchanged as we engage in the pastime of talking about our hopes and wishes.

- If you put something off for long enough, someone else might do it for you. In this way procrastination can become a method of controlling other people.

- Delaying when you have a deadline so that you leave yourself the minimum amount of time means that you have an

139

excuse for making mistakes or doing sloppy work: 'I just didn't have enough time to check it as well as I wanted to.'

Exercise: Having read the above, look over your own list of things you are putting off and identify the possible benefit you are gaining from the delay.

Having completed the exercises, you may now have some insight into why you are delaying. Here are some ways you can challenge yourself to get out of the procrastination trap;

- Sit down and get started on something you have been putting off. Begin to write a letter or read a book. You will discover that putting this off has been largely unnecessary since the activity is likely to be more pleasurable than you anticipated. If it isn't, at least you will have the satisfaction of knowing that you are doing something that has to be done. You no longer have to think anxious thoughts about getting it over with!

- Ask yourself, 'What is the worst thing that could happen if I do this?' Lay out your fears and assess them. You may find that the thing you fear is not so great after all. For instance, sometimes the answer to the question is; 'That nothing will change'. If the worst thing that can happen is that things stay the same, what have you got to lose by taking action? Nothing!

- Try the experiment of living five minutes at a time, instead of always thinking in the long term. For the next five minutes do something that you want, refusing to respond to anything that would delay you. Concentrate fully on what you are doing, staying aware of how you are thinking and feeling. At the end of the five minutes, consider what you have achieved. You may be surprised at the amount you can do in such a short time span, provided you allow yourself to get on with it.

- Give yourself a specific time slot (say, tomorrow between 9.00 and 9.30 a.m.) for doing something which you have been delaying. Write it in your diary and don't let yourself be distracted. Don't spend more or less time than you decided upon.

- Make your mind work for you when you get bored. Challenge yourself to find interest and stimulation at such times. At meetings, for instance, if you usually don't have too much to contribute, ask a question or make a point. Or use your mind in different ways – set yourself mental arithmetic puzzles, make up a crossword. On tedious journeys, make up a story about your fellow travellers, do some homework, write a poem, practise lightning sketches – in fact anything that will keep your mind exercised.

- Stop something now! If there is something you know you should give up – make the decision to do it now! If you are anxious about the effects of your smoking, drinking, drug-taking and the like, take action now. If you are a smoker who wants to stop, put the book down, collect up your cigarettes and throw them away. If you are a drinker who wants to stop, pour any drink you have in the house away. Don't think about it – just do it. If problems arise as a result of your action, deal with them when they come up rather than letting the thought of them prevent you. As far as I know, not many people die as a result of giving up smoking, drinking or other dangerous addictions!

- Start something now! If you have been thinking about starting a diet, begin now. If you are due for a snack – eat an apple instead of a biscuit. Start your exercise programme. Take a couple of deep breaths, put the book down, stand up and stretch, bend slowly to touch your toes – see? It's easier than you thought. The first problem is over, now all you have to do is continue.

- Be brave about doing something that you have been avoiding because you are afraid of not doing it well enough. Take a chance – do it as well as you can now; you can always decide to learn or practise more to improve on your performance. But if you don't take the risk, you won't know what needs working on.

- Think again about the idea of only having a short time to

live. What are you putting off that you would regret under those circumstances? Think hard about how much longer you want to delay. At what point will it be the right time? Do you actually KNOW how much longer you will live?

- If you feel too tired to do something you have been putting off, check whether you actually are physically fatigued – in which case explore any possible ways of changing your life-style so that you are able to increase your energy. More sleep? Better diet? Does your tiredness 'magically' disappear when you turn to something else? This is a sign that your tiredness might be an unconscious tactic to help you avoid the risks that go with the action.

- Delete the words 'maybe', 'hopefully', 'wish' from your vocabulary. Just using the words helps you to delay longer. Experiment with changing 'hopefully things will work out' to 'I will make things work'; 'I wish I could make things better' to 'This is what I am going to do to make things better'; 'Maybe it'll happen one day' to 'I'm going to start today'.

- If there is something between you and other people that you are avoiding – arrange a meeting between all involved. Explain that you want to do something to change things – but you can't do it on your own. Talk about your feelings, fears and worries and ask for their reaction. If it would help you to rehearse with someone, enlist the help of a friend. However difficult the problems between you are, they will be easier to deal with if they are out in the open. If you keep it all in your head, the anxieties will continue to grow. In Chapters 10 and 11 you will find some practical ideas for approaching difficult situations.

- Write out a contract stating clearly what you intend to stop putting off. If other people are involved, give them a copy so they can hold you to it.

- Put notices up wherever you will be able to see them with messages like 'DO IT NOW!'

This chapter has encouraged you to challenge any delaying tactics you have been using to put off making important changes. If you are serious about wanting to change the way you are using your time, begin to do those things which you know will have some effect. If you decide not to go ahead, be clear that this is a decision you are making and for which you are responsible. Then put the matter out of your head and use your energy for things that you are intending to do.

In the next chapter you will have a chance to focus further on how to raise your awareness of thinking patterns which may stand in the way of your progress.

9

KEEP YOUR HEAD

When we think of time, we often think in terms of the past, present and future. The past has, of course, already gone and there is nothing at all we can do to change it. The future is something we can wonder about and plan for but it hasn't happened yet. The one thing we do have with absolute certainty is the present. This chapter is about how the way we think can spoil the present for us.

Here is a story showing how an idea about the future can ruin the present. Once upon a time, Mary wanted to bake a cake. She gathered together all the ingredients but discovered that she didn't have the right kind of sugar. She thought about knocking next door and borrowing some from her neighbour, Jenny. She started walking down the garden path towards Jenny's door. She was thinking, 'Jenny has never borrowed anything from me – she always seems well organized. She probably hates people borrowing things. I bet she'll think that I'm terribly inefficient not to have enough sugar. She'll probably tell everyone that I ran out. All the neighbours will know. I'll never be able to hold my head up in front of them.' As she reached the door, Jenny opened it, smiled and said, 'Hi! How nice to see you. What can I do for you?' Mary shouted, 'I can manage perfectly well without your sugar, thank you very much. I don't need anything from you at all! In fact, I don't need anything from anybody.'

This is an example of how it's possible to take an idea, work on it, create a fantasy and act on the fantasy as if it were real. It introduces this chapter which is about your relationship with yourself. You, after all, are the person that you spend most time with. You have been with you all your life and know yourself better than anyone. This is one relationship which it will pay to get right.

Mirror, Mirror . . .

Many of the exercises in this book are designed to allow you to learn more about yourself; the more you learn, the more chance you stand of changing the things that you want to be different. The effect of some of the exercises is like holding up a mirror so that you can see yourself. Here is an exercise which enables you to have a good look at yourself:

> *Exercise: Sit or stand in front of the largest mirror you have. You can keep your clothes on or take them off. Have a really good look at yourself. First, look at your physical self; how is your body looking? If you want to experiment with this exercise you could imagine asking each part of your body how it's getting on; what it wants from you; how it would like to be treated differently and so on.*
>
> *Before moving on, jot down your reactions so far. Then think about the skills you have. Look at your image in the mirror and say to yourself, 'You are a person who is good at . . . (fill in the details yourself); you are a person who wants to change . . . and to learn . . . (again fill in the details)'.*
>
> *The next stage is to say to yourself, 'So far in your life you have achieved . . . (fill in the details); you want to go on to achieve . . . (fill in the details)'.*
>
> *You can finish the exercise by saying to yourself, '. . . (your name) – you are special because . . .'*

This exercise is a very good one to do on a regular basis as a way of reminding yourself who you are, what you are trying to achieve and what you have already achieved in life. It is a way of encouraging you to think positively about yourself even though there are things about yourself that you are not satisfied with and want to change.

Who's Writing the Script?

It is important to spend some time being conscious of ourselves through awareness of our thoughts and feelings. One of the reasons that it's important to consider this is that thoughts can become self-fulfilling prophecies. It is as if once we have identified our worst worry, we actually become more vulnerable. It is too simple and glib to say that positive thinking can cure every problem – but on the other hand it is foolish to ignore the power of thought completely.

Most theories of psychological development place emphasis on the effect of childhood experience on our adult life-patterns, and in previous chapters we have alluded to the way that as children we create our perception of the world. Eric Berne, whose ideas about strokes and games we have already explored, formulated a theory that as children we lay down a specific plan for our lives – a script. This script, he suggested, is laid out in the form of a drama with a clear-cut beginning, middle and end. As adults, we are likely to remain unaware of the early decisions we made, even though we may be living them out in our behaviour. Here are some exercises which give you the opportunity to test out the idea for yourself.

In an earlier exercise you considered your life as a drama. These exercises draw further on dreams, fairy-tales and childhood stories which may well give clues to your script.

Let your imagination run free when you are doing these exercises. Don't worry too much about what they mean or what you are supposed to say. Accept the first images which come to you and notice any feelings which accompany them. Interpreting can be done afterwards.

You could do the exercises with a partner or a group; if you are alone you could record your responses. Just turn on a tape recorder and leave it running. When you play it back you may be surprised at the amount you learn about yourself and your script.

One more point before you begin. You may during any of the exercises experience quite strong emotions. Perhaps memories will surface which upset you in some way. If this happens, it's OK to stop the exercise. If you are working with someone else, explain what is happening. Allow yourself to calm down by doing one of the breathing exercises and focusing your attention on something else. You can then explore the implications of the effect at your own pace.

Exercise 1: Do you have a favourite hero or heroine? Perhaps someone from a childhood story or a play, book or film you remember. Choose the first character that comes to mind. Talk or write about yourself as if you were this person. Speak in the first person, using the word 'I'. For example, 'I am Robin Hood. I like helping people. I have chosen to live outside the law because I believe in justice. I am able to hide in the woods and am very independent . . .'

Exercise 2: Retell a favourite childhood story, myth or fable. Do this from your memory without referring to a book. For instance, 'Once upon a time there was a girl who loved her parents but her mother died. Her father married a horrible woman who had two daughters who were very ugly. The girl was very unhappy because her father no longer seemed to love her and the stepmother and her daughters treated the girl very badly. She became a servant and had to work hard and no-one knew how unhappy she was because she was so diligent . . .'

A variation is to re-tell the story several times from the point of view of different characters. 'I'm Cinderella's step-sister. I know deep down that I'm ugly and clumsy but if I act as if I don't care then no-one will know . . .'

Exercise 3: Choose a recent dream you have had. Tell the dream as if it were happening now. Just like the previous exercise, tell the dream from the point of view of the events and characters in it. Make up different endings until you find one with which you are fully satisfied.

Exercise 4: Look around the room you are in at the

147

moment. Choose any object you can see. Now pre-
tend to be that object and talk about yourself. 'I'm
the chair. I'm well worn and people sit on me all
the time. I know that people think I'm comfortable
but I don't think that anyone really notices me ...'

Whatever you write or say in response to these exercises will reveal something of your inner world. If you are doing them with another person, he or she can help you explore how your answers may show aspects of your life script. You might notice certain patterns. Eric Berne identified six very common ones:

Until: If you are living out an Until script your motto in life is likely to be: 'I can't have fun *until* I've finished my work.' There are many variations like, 'I can't change until I've fully understood myself'; 'Life doesn't really begin until you're thirty/forty/fifty/married/rich/ . . .'; 'You can't expect any reward until you get to Heaven'. The trouble with this idea is that you can't really get on with your life until whatever it is you are waiting for happens. A script pattern can emerge in events, like not letting yourself sit down to enjoy a TV programme until you've done the washing up. Its influence, though, may be felt on larger life issues, like not committing yourself to an intimate relationship or changing a job until you feel you are certain that every contingency is covered.

When he identified these script themes, Berne linked each one to one of the ancient myths of gods and goddesses, heroes and heroines. You may remember the Greek heroes Hercules, Theseus and Jason. Each of them had to undertake arduous tasks before they could reach a state of happiness. Hercules undertook twelve tasks which included destroying the Hydra, a hundred-headed serpent and cleaning out the Augean stables; Theseus had to kill the Minotaur before his true identity was accepted; Jason was denied his kingdom until he brought back the Golden Fleece.

Gavin is a modern-day example of someone with this kind of script. He often says, 'When the children grow up and leave, I'll have all the time I want to relax and do things I've always wanted to do.' He is ignoring the possibility of getting enjoyment and satisfaction from doing at least some of these things now. In this scenario, there is also the risk of the children eventually being blamed for limiting his freedom; perhaps they will be expected to make up for the sacrifice in some way.

After: This pattern is the opposite of the Until script. Someone with this script follows the motto: 'If I have fun today, I'll have to pay for it tomorrow'; 'Having children is great, but once you have them you lose most of your independence'; 'The weather is wonderful this morning, but we're bound to pay for it with rain this evening' are all expressions of the After script. The big problem for this person is that he or she can never fully enjoy the present moment. Part of their mind is always concerned with how they will have to pay.

Another Greek myth illustrates this script pattern – that of Damocles. He actually had a very good lifestyle – eating, drinking and generally making merry. But all the time there was a sword suspended on a single horse-hair above his head. Once he saw it, he could never be happy again. He lived in constant fear of when the hair would break and the sword would come down on his neck.

Jennifer has an After script. It affects her in small ways like if she is having a good time at a party, she will be worrying about a hangover in the morning. It also affects her life in more major ways. For instance, she has had several intimate relationships, but so far they have always foundered because as soon as she feels she is becoming more committed, worries about the future take over. She feels an increasing dread that some disaster will overtake her and her partner and so she feels it is safer to let the relationship drift.

Never: The theme of this script is 'I will never get what I most want.' Typical expressions of this pattern: 'I'd really like to get married, but I'd never be able to find anyone who would live with me'; 'I've tried hard to get on but I'll never get promotion'; 'I'd like to go back to college but they'd never accept someone like me'.

Tantalus is the Greek hero who personifies this script pattern. He was confined to a lake but when thirst overcame him the water receded so that he could not drink. When he was hungry he would try to pick fruit from the branch hanging just above his head which would rise just out of reach. Tantalus was confined by the Gods and so presumably couldn't move out of the lake on his own initiative. Someone with a Never script may feel life is like this and so accept that there is nothing they can do to change things. But they may well be able to take a step to move closer to what they want if they are willing to take responsibility.

Alice says she would like to settle down in a steady relationship with a man, but she has never done so. Her job gives her many opportunities to meet new people and she has lots of acquaintances. However she never seems to have time to devote to making and maintaining a lasting relationship. She often talks about how she should organize things differently, but in fact does nothing about it. She feels confined in much the same way as Tantulus was captive.

Always: The classic question asked by this script-owner is 'Why does this always happen to me?' Repetition is the most obvious evidence that this is the dominant script theme. Someone with this script may play it out by going from one unsatisfactory relationship, job or place to another. Or they may express it by staying in an unsatisfactory situation instead of changing things or moving on. Typical responses would be: 'I've been going to this counsellor for years but I don't seem to get anything out of it'; 'You've made your bed, now you must lie on it'; 'I don't know how I'm always the one who gets left out'.

The mythical figure for this script pattern is Arachne. She was exceptionally skilled at embroidery and not at all modest about her talent. She went so far as to challenge the goddess Athena to a competition. Athena was so outraged that she turned Arachne into a spider and condemned her to spin her web for all eternity.

Beatrice has been married twice. Her first husband was very possessive and demanded her attention one hundred percent. She was very unhappy because she felt imprisoned in the relationship. She finally left her husband saying that she wanted to be free and independent. Within six months she had started another relationship with a man who was very much like her first husband. She married him and again became very unhappy, feeling trapped in another unsatisfactory marriage. The marriage didn't last long. Beatrice's friends are amazed that she has started a third relationship with someone very similar and is talking about getting married again.

Zachary is a teacher in a large inner-city secondary school. He loves teaching but feels more and more oppressed by the structure and atmosphere in the school in which he has taught for fifteen years. He often talks about his unhappiness with the way things are going for him. Friends have suggested that he look around for another school but he says that he doesn't see how he can move now.

Almost: The motto for this script could be 'I almost made it this time.' Someone influenced by this particular pattern would be for ever starting things but very rarely finishing them. Sisyphus is the model for this script.

By now you will have realized that the Ancient Greek Gods were a touchy lot. Sisyphus, like very many others, fell foul of them. His punishment was to roll an enormous rock up a slope which, when it reached the top, rolled down to the bottom and Sisyphus' task began at the beginning again. This is how life feels to someone with the Almost script – they just feel they are getting to where they want to be and something happens, so they have to start all over again. A variation of the pattern is where the person does actually make it to the top, but instead of relaxing and enjoying the achievement, looks around for an even higher peak to climb.

Wendy has a house full of unfinished projects; paintings not quite completed; books half-read; knitted jumpers waiting to be sewn up and so on. She is a very competent manager of a small department. She has applied for promotion and several times got short-listed. But she can't seem to quite make it to the top of the ladder.

Gillian has got to the top of the tree in her particular field as a well respected consultant in medicine. However, she is not resting on her laurels. She is now writing a text book and planning to conduct some new research. She is admired and sometimes envied by her friends but she herself doesn't feel she has succeeded.

Open-Ended: This pattern can resemble any of the other scripts until a certain cut-off point when things begin to change. For the person with this script the time after the cut-off is a void. It is as if the closing pages of the play have gone missing. The motto would be something like, 'Once I get to a certain point, I won't know what to do with myself afterwards'. This point could be retirement, children leaving home, a certain age, death of a partner and so on.

Once again, there is a mythical example. Philemon and Baucis were an elderly couple. They pleased the gods, who had taken the form of travel-worn strangers, by welcoming them when others would not. Their reward was to have their lives extended by being turned into trees planted beside each other with their branches entwined. They believed they could not live without each other and so they were never left alone.

When his wife died, William felt his own life had ended. It is four years after her death, but he stays in the house becoming more and more depressed. He resists any attempt by friends to help him create a satisfying life for himself. He has no interest in caring for himself and is not eating or sleeping well. It is as if he has decided that there is no life for him now.

Vera was looking forward to her children leaving home. She thought that she would enjoy liberation from the various trials and tribulations of parenting five lively children. But a very short time after the last child moved out she is feeling at a loose end. She doesn't really know what to do with all her time and thinks nostalgically about being so busy that she didn't have time to think at all.

A Mixture of Scripts: Many people identify with one or other of these six patterns and it's probably true to say that most of us have elements of all the scripts. However there is often one theme which is dominant.

Some of us combine two of the scripts. Gillian mentioned above, for instance, is a mixture of Almost and Until. She seems to be telling herself: 'I can't rest until I've reached the top. But I'll never be able to make it to the top because there's always a higher peak to climb. I'll never be able to rest.' If you combined Never and Until you would be telling yourself: 'I can't enjoy myself until I've finished work. But I'll never finish work – so I'll never have fun.'

From these examples you will see how easily we can trap ourselves in these patterns of thinking.

> *Exercise: Having read through the descriptions of the six script patterns, pick out those which seem typical of you. How do you act your script out? Are you satisfied with the patterns you have identified?*

Changing the Script:

If you are uncomfortable with your script you can change it. The previous exercise will help you to begin by identifying patterns which you weren't clearly aware of before. Once you have done this, you need to decide what would be necessary to take control and break through the patterns. Here are some practical examples:

If your main pattern has been Until, change things by deliberately going ahead and having fun even before you have finished all your work. If you are cleaning the house, why not do half and then give yourself a treat – go for a walk, read a chapter of your novel, make a cup of coffee, watch a programme on TV or whatever would please you. Then continue with the cleaning.

If you are someone with an After script, think about what would be necessary for you to enjoy tomorrow as well as today and behave accordingly. For instance, if you're going on holiday, making time to finish up tasks so that you will not be worried about the amount of work waiting for you when you get home. If you are going to a party, decide in advance on the amount you can drink safely and don't go over the limit. In this way your worry-type thinking becomes redundant.

Breaking out of the Never script is simply a question of clarifying what you want. Decide on the goals which would help you achieve what you want and write them down. Do one thing on your list each day. If you want to improve your education, but up to now have assumed that you could never do it, go along to your local Further Education College and discuss what you want. You will find that there are many approaches now to continuing education and it is very likely that there is a structure that would be appropriate for you.

If you feel caught in an Always script, identify one thing where what you are continually doing does not solve the problem. Now do something different. If you, for instance, are stuck in an unhappy relationship and have been keeping quiet, communicate your thoughts and feelings to the other person. If you are in a job which is unsatisfying, look for something new.

The Almost script is best demolished by finishing things. You can start with small things. If you start a book – finish it. If you set out to write a letter, make sure you finish it and send it off. It can be very rewarding to record your own achievements perhaps by making a list. This is just to remind you that you are succeeding in fulfilling your ambitions and that you can afford to rest from time to time. When you start off on something new, check whether it is something you really want to do or is it something you feel driven to do.

If you think you have an Open-Ended script, take some time to write a satisfying ending.

These changes are not as easy to make as they are to write about. You are bound to feel uncomfortable and perhaps even silly as you actually behave in unfamiliar ways but it's worth it. You will get a sense of control over yourself that you may never have had before. Use the ideas in the chapter on Goal Setting to help you and remember that each time you behave in a way that contradicts your script you are weakening the pattern. In time, you will have written a new script.

Much of what we have explored requires a high level of self-observation. To develop your ability, ask yourself these questions at regular intervals during the day:

      What am I thinking now?
      What am I doing now?
      What am I feeling now?

As you answer these questions in your mind, you may become aware of a pattern developing and this will be the chance to cut across it. For instance, supposing you woke up on a sunny day and found yourself thinking 'It's nice now but it's bound to rain this afternoon'. A familiar gloom might then descend on your feelings and you'd notice your face fall and your shoulders drop. Just another dreary day! This sounds like a typical After script. As you notice these things, you could change what you think. This isn't as difficult as it might sound. If you doubt the possibility of controlling your thinking try this exercise:

> *Exercise: Since this is one of those exercises that requires you to close your eyes, you'll have to read it all to begin with and then do it. Or you can get a friend to read it out loud and take you through the steps.*
>
> *Close your eyes and imagine a pink elephant. Take time for this. Really conjure up the image in your mind and imagine yourself looking at it from all angles.*
>
> *Now change this imagine into a green lion. Again, take time and don't worry if it doesn't come easily. If you persist, you will be able to create the second image.*
>
> *Now change the image back into the pink elephant again. Take whatever time it takes – just persist until you have succeeded.*
>
> *Now play around with the images. Turn from one to the other at will. You will find that it becomes easier with practice.*

The next question to ask yourself is: What do I really want for myself now?

Sometimes when you are in the grip of a script pattern you may find it difficult to let go even though your answer to the question is: 'To relax and find another way to behave'. If this is the case you need to ask yourself: 'What am I gaining from this behaviour? What is my investment in continuing it?' You may find that it supports an element of your script as it has been up to now; that it feels 'natural' even though it doesn't lead you to be happy or satisfied. In this case you need to divert your thinking. The previous exercise wouldn't work if you were just told not to think of the pink elephant. It's impossible *not* to think of something. What does work is replacing the unwanted thought with a positive substitute.

We are always doing something in our mind – working out a problem, thinking, planning for the future, imagining, anticipating, remembering something from the past, judging. But it's surprising how little we are really aware of what we are doing. The next time you are with someone who seems to have gone 'into themselves', ask them what they were thinking. You will find that many people can't really tell you – they just know they were 'thinking'.

Try this exercise for yourself to identify what you are thinking about now:

> *Exercise: Make sure you won't be interrupted for about 30 minutes. Sit comfortably and have a piece of paper and a pen ready. Close your eyes and concentrate on your breathing. As you sit, thoughts will come to you – as they do, open your eyes and jot down a label for the particular thought. Let that thought go out of your mind, concentrate on your breathing again and wait for the next thought.*

Now look at your list. You might have thoughts about the environment – too hot, too cold, noises you notice and so on. You may have been aware of something in your body – a pain, tension or some other sensation. You may have spent time in the future, planning or listing things you need to do. Some thoughts may have been about the past – something left undone or some pleasant memory. Maybe you thought about a particular person. You may be surprised at the range of your thinking – or perhaps you notice that it is rather limited. Did you, for instance, spend most time in the past – or in the present? Perhaps one thought took over, making it difficult for you to clear your mind.

It is a good discipline to tune into your mind regularly to become aware of what you are thinking. In this way you can pay attention to how your thoughts are helping or hindering you.

When you notice yourself moving into familiar script-type thinking you can check whether these thoughts are really about the present moment or whether they are just habits from the past.

A Cast of Thousands? Well, probably not thousands! However, many people experience their minds as battlegrounds with different voices trying to take control. For instance, Ruth is a mature student, studying at the same time as bringing up her children. She might hear one voice saying: 'You've got an essay to write. You need to get it finished today so that you have time to go over it and check the references.' But just as she gets ready to start she might hear, 'You haven't done the ironing yet and the kids need clean clothes for school tomorrow.' And another, 'You haven't had a night off for ages. You're entitled to some fun. The others are all going to the cinema and you could go with them. All work and no play will make you into a very boring person.' Then another voice makes itself heard: 'It's all wasted because you're just not clever enough to succeed.'

In fact many psychologists have written about the way that our personality takes on different aspects, each representing a different need. Roberto Assagioli devised the idea of thinking of each voice as a sub-personality which would be given a name. Ruth calls the first voice 'Responsible Ruth', the second 'The Housewife'; the third 'Good Time Ruthy' and the fourth 'The Underminer'.

Each voice represents a need. Responsible Ruth gives voice to that part of her which wants to succeed and progress; The Housewife is afraid that she will let things go and the children will suffer if she concentrates too much on her studies; Good Time Ruthy is the part of her that resents not being able to relax and enjoy herself like her friends and the Underminer represents her doubts and uncertainties regarding her ability to succeed.

> *Exercise: Make a list of your wants; whatever comes to mind. Your list can include things that you haven't got yet and also things that you have got now and want to continue having.*

e.g. I want to be healthy
to have friends
to be respected
to get a degree
to be a good parent
to make lots of money
to have a partner to love
to learn to swim
and so on.

When you are satisfied with the list – select the six which are most important. You might want to group some together: for instance, losing weight, taking exercise, stopping smoking could come under the heading, 'To be more healthy'.

On a large sheet of paper, draw an image to represent each want and then give each image a name. These are your sub-personalities.

If you are interested in this idea, you could develop it further. For instance you can imagine conversations between the various sub-personalities, particularly those which are in conflict. The more you get to know them, the easier it will be to control their influence. Sometimes you can do a deal. Ruth promised 'Good Time Ruthy' an outing if she would stay quiet when 'Responsible Ruth' was working. Housewife Ruth conceded that sometimes her needs were not the most important to fulfil right away. The Underminer realized that the idea that she was not capable really came from the past and that she was proving over and over again that she had the ability to succeed.

The point of these exercises is to provide you with a device to make you more in control of your thoughts so that you don't unnecessarily sabotage your efforts to change. The Saboteur is a very common sub-personality and has a way of emerging just when you are about to do something important. Here is an exercise to help you identify your own Saboteur:

Exercise: Think about something that you would like to achieve. Examples might be learning to swim, cooking a gourmet meal, passing an exam. Now visualize yourself achieving this project.

Notice whether any thoughts intrude on the picture of success. Maybe you begin to think about how the project might fail or how something might destroy it.

These thoughts are the voice of your Saboteur. If you like working with images, draw a picture of the Saboteur in action. Or you can imagine the Saboteur actually damaging your project.

The next step is to imagine yourself confronting and negotiating with the Saboteur.

Talking to Yourself: We've spent some time in this chapter exploring the power of positive thought; let's now consider how positive thinking can be converted into positive talking. We know that negative thinking can really stand in the way of progress and development. Positive self-talking will help you through situations where the Saboteur is waiting to pounce. This chapter ends with some common situations where what we tell ourselves will affect our performance. If you know that you are likely to be telling yourself something from the 'negative self-talk' side, try replacing it from the 'positive self-talk' side.

Preparing for Something You Expect to be Stressful:

Positive Self-Talk	*Negative Self-Talk*
How shall I prepare for this?	I'll never be able to do this.
I do feel afraid, but I'm going ahead.	It's too frightening.
I'm as well prepared as I can be. If there's something that I don't know, I'll ask for time to find out.	They're bound to catch me out.

159

Coping With Anxiety:

I can feel the anxiety growing; I'll breathe slowly and relax my muscles.

It's stupid to be anxious.

I can manage this.

I'll never be able to manage this.

It's natural to feel fear.

I shouldn't feel afraid.

When You Are Disappointed At How You've Performed:

I didn't do as well as I wanted, but I did my best and that's what counts.

I should have done better.

These are the ways I succeeded and these are the ways I failed.

I wasn't successful.

This is what I would do differently next time.

I'm never going to do that again.

I did what I felt was right for me at the time. If others are upset with me, I can cope with that.

I shouldn't have hurt their feelings.

I am getting better at this.

I'll never be able to do it.

When You Are Angry:

What do I want to achieve?

I've got to win.

It might not be necessary to argue.

There's bound to be an argument.

I need to find out what the other person wants.

I'll get one up as soon as I can.

There's nothing for me to prove.

I'll show them.

160

What does he/she want? He/she's wrong.

How can we both benefit? He/she's against me.

All the above are examples of how you can replace a potentially destructive thought with one that will help you to keep your aims in view.

> *Exercise: Remember the last time you were in a difficult or stressful situation. Were there any thoughts in your head which hindered rather than helped you at the time? Can you see how you might replace any of them?*

Saying 'Yes' To Yourself

We have seen how a negative view of yourself can become a self-fulfilling prophecy and have explored different ways of getting out of the destructive circle of thoughts which can affect how we behave. The previous section suggests that we can consciously use our thoughts to help us succeed. Autosuggestion or 'affirmations' is a method which develops this idea and is used successfully by many people. It works on the basis of deciding on a positive view of yourself and then telling yourself over and over that it is true. Although you may think it sounds too simple to be effective, it might be worth your while to experiment for a while to see whether this is a method which works for you.

> *Exercise: You need to decide what aspect of your life you want to improve in this way and then create the appropriate affirmation. For example, 'I want a better relationship with . . ./I want to be better tempered/I want to be more healthy/relaxed/ courageous and so on.'*
>
> *When you have decided on your goal, write it out on a card as if you had succeeded.*
>
> *e.g. I (your name) am clever enough to understand . . .*
>
> *I . . . am able to forgive . . .*

161

I ... have the will-power to keep my diet

I ... am confident

I ... am entitled to speak up at meetings

I ... am an attractive person

I ... am working on the manuscript and will finish it on time and so on.

You will notice that all the affirmations are stated as positives ('I am confident' rather than 'I am not afraid') and that they can be very general or specific.

These affirmations are a way of saying 'yes' to yourself and the idea is to repeat them at least ten times a day. You can look at yourself in a mirror while you read them out; you can record them on a tape and play them to yourself in the car, in bed at night or when you wake up in the morning.

However sceptical you are – give it a try. After all, the worst that can happen is that you hear a few nice things about yourself!

This section has concentrated on your relationship with yourself; now we will explore some of the issues which arise when we spend time with other people.

10

TIME FOR QUALITY

Imagine that you are visiting a place called Nowhere. This is a spot where nothing living exists. There are no animals, no birds, no people, not even any plants. You are travelling alone, with nothing and you have just arrived. There is no sound, no form, no colour. For many people this is an unpleasant and frightening exercise. For one thing, it is difficult to keep a sense of identity because there are no reference points. You know you exist but how do you know what that means in a world with no reference points?

The point of this exercise is to demonstrate how important other people are to us. It is through our relationships with others that we define ourselves. If you are one of those people who is completely satisfied and happy living the life of a hermit, skip this chapter. If, on the other hand, you want to increase or improve the quality of the important relationships in your life, read on. We are going to explore how to make more of the time spent with other people.

In Chapter 3 we explored the different levels of relationship based on the depth of the contact between the people. Now our focus is on quality and is about the time we spend in those relationships which give us most potential for intimate contact. Intimate contact, you will recall, is where we feel safe enough to drop the defences or 'masks' we develop to protect us as we go through life. These are the relationships where you can be yourself without having to pretend; where you are acceptable and accepting. These are our quality relationships.

There are certain people in our life with whom we have a close connection and the chance to develop high quality relationships;

our mothers, fathers, grandparents and other members of the family in which we are born. Then there are the people that we meet during our lifetime; teachers, colleagues, lovers, husbands, wives, friends and so on.

> *Exercise: Make a list of the people in your life with whom you might have a loving, intimate relationship. Don't censure your list so that you only include those with whom you already have a good relationship. This is an exercise in identifying the potential as well as actual. As you make your list, listen to your thoughts particularly about the people with whom you do not have a satisfactory association at the moment. On what is your judgement based? A long past event? Gossip? An unchecked perception? If so perhaps you need to review your judgement.*

Defining a loving relationship is not as simple as it seems. You certainly know when you haven't got it; it's more difficult to know clearly what it is so that you can go about creating one.

As far as I'm concerned, a loving relationship is one in which you feel personally touched by the other person; in which you are emotionally affected by them. You might feel respectful, loving, affectionate towards them or you might dislike, disregard or even hate them. The one thing you won't feel is neutral. This, incidentally, is why it is so difficult to react objectively to such people. A friend of mine said recently, 'I just don't understand it. I'm a trained counsellor; I am good at helping my clients to overcome some of the problems in their lives – but I just can't get on with my mother! I know that I'm doing exactly the things that make things worse between us – and I'd certainly encourage a client to behave differently – but I can't do it myself.' The stronger the connection the greater our investment in the relationship. The greater our investment, the more likely we are to continue repeating patterns that maintain the status quo. Changing how we react requires us to stand back and detach ourselves from that investment. No easy task!

Creating and maintaining good relationships is one of the keys to happiness. Much more important than any kind of material comforts or a brilliant career. To love and be loved in return provides a wonderful feeling of well-being that can affect the whole of our life. The strength and confidence that comes from such relationships can sustain us through difficult times and many problems. But loving relationships need attention.

Five Fine Gifts

Do you remember the beginning of the story of Sleeping Beauty? She was the much longed-for daughter of a King and Queen. At her christening, each good fairy presented her with a gift which would contribute to a happy healthy life. Supposing you were that baby – what gifts would you hope for? Including the following five attributes in your list would certainly help you to make the most of your personal relationships:

The gift of good listening This would enable you to listen and understand what another person is saying.

The gift of expressing yourself This one would mean that you would be able to put your thoughts and feelings into words so that others were able to understand you.

The gift of assertion Being given this would enable you to be respected and to satisfy your needs without abusing, oppressing or controlling other people.

The gift of facing conflicts With this you would be able to face conflict head on in a constructive way so that whatever the result, your relationship would not suffer.

The gift of solving problems Having this would mean that you would be able to solve problems so that all parties were satisfied.

These gifts would prepare you well to meet most of the communication difficulties which arise in personal relationships. But if you weren't visited with these talents at birth, don't despair. We'll consider each one and explore ways of giving them to yourself.

Gift No. 1: Listening Is More Than Just Hearing The Words

The quality of our friendships, family relationships and effectiveness at work is heavily influenced by our listening skill. It may seem strange that something most of us do so naturally needs skill, but it certainly does. Good listening is more than just being quiet while someone is talking. Think of the last time you were in the company of someone who wasn't a good listener. Can you remember the effect on you? Did you feel angry or frustrated because you were trying to get a particular message across? Were you bored because the person was only interested in getting their message across to you? Maybe you felt discounted and unimportant because you got no response. However you were affected, it is likely you felt bad in some way.

There is a difference between *hearing* and *listening*. Have you ever been at a party where a lot of talking is going on. One person is telling the story of an event they experienced; someone else is grumbling about their job, while another person is jubilant about a new job. In another corner, someone else is describing the symptoms of their latest illness. As you look round you could get the sense that no-one is really listening to anyone. People look as if they are but their eyes are wandering around the room; maybe they are rehearsing their own stories, waiting for a chance to tell them or checking to see if there is someone who looks more interesting to talk to. The party feels like a great success, but most people will go home without really knowing each other. They have heard each other's words, but not really listened to the meanings.

Here are a set of exercises designed to point to the effects of low quality listening. They are intended to be done with a partner because we are exploring communicating with other people. You may already have someone who is joining you in experimenting with the exercises – if not make an attempt now to set up some practice with a friend. Explaining the point of the exercise can give you a good reason for taking the initiative to create a new friendship or deepen an existing one.

Exercise 1: You will need a minute timer for these exercises. Set the timer for five minutes. Sit facing each other and begin a conversation. You are bound to feel a bit self-conscious so don't worry about it. You can start by talking about that if you wish. When the five minutes are up, share your reactions with each other. How easy/difficult was it to keep the conversation going? Who took the initiative? How did it feel when the timer interrupted?

Exercise 2: Now set the timer for three minutes and turn your chairs back to back. Conduct the conversation in this position. When the time is up, once again discuss the effect. What was it like to be cut off from visual contact? Did you notice yourself making any compensations for not being able to see? Did you find yourself distracted by your surroundings?

Exercise 3: Turn the chairs round and set the timer for three minutes. This time one of you will stand up (or stand on the chair) while the other sits on the floor or on a chair. Keep eye contact with each other and continue the conversation. When the timer goes, change positions and continue talking for another three minutes. When the time is up, discuss the effects. Did you feel more powerful when you were higher than the other person? Did this affect how you communicated? Did you feel different when you were in the lower position? How did this affect you?

Exercise 4: Now stand up and face each other. Set the timer for three minutes. Talk to each other with each of you looking over the other's shoulder. When the time is up, discuss how you felt. Did you do anything to try to get eye contact with your partner? Did you lose interest?

Exercise 5: In this exercise, continue standing facing each other. The first person looks over the head of the other, making no eye contact. The other looks directly at the partner. After three minutes, reverse positions. Discuss your reactions.

Exercise 6: Continuing the pattern, stand and face

each other but this time stand at least twelve feet apart. When you discuss your reactions, check whether this has felt at all familiar. Did the distance between you change what you chose to talk about?

Exercise 7: Now come back together and sit face to face. This time hold up a large sheet of paper or put a screen between you. What were your thoughts and feelings while doing this? Again, did you feel anything was familiar?

Exercise 8: Sitting in the same positions, the first person looks at him or herself in a hand mirror. The second person looks at the first person directly, not in the mirror. After three minutes reverse roles and then discuss the experience with each other.

Exercise 9: This is the last one in the series, so you should sit comfortably, make eye contact and hold hands if you wish. Sit quietly for a moment, thinking about what has happened and then talk with each other about your reactions and what you might have learnt about communication.

These exercises will have shown up some of the ways in which listening gets marred. Good listening is an essential skill for making and keeping relationships. If you're a good listener, you'll notice that others are drawn to you. Your ability to listen helps you to know what people want and what might hurt or irritate them. People feel you understand them and confide in you so your friendships deepen.

On the other hand, people who don't listen often find themselves feeling lonely and isolated. Being a bad listener means giving the message: 'What you have to say doesn't matter much to me.' Potential colleagues, friends or lovers are turned off because you only seem interested in yourself.

Time can be wasted because of bad listening! You miss important information and so don't see problems approaching. Clues about people's state of mind pass you by so that misunderstandings can occur.

Listening with Intent

We are listening at our best when our definite intention is to understand or enjoy someone; to learn something; or to give help or comfort to someone. If we are doing any of these things, we can't help but listen carefully because our attention is turned on the other person. Our own needs are put in second place.

There are bound to be times when, although you are hearing the words, you are not really listening. For example, whenever you are listening:

- hoping that you will be seen as a good, kind person;
- to check whether the person likes you;
- for the other to stop so that you can say what you want;
- for any flaws in the other person's argument so that you will be proved right;
- because you don't know how to end the conversation or get away;
- with the worry that you may be rejected;
- to produce a particular effect;
- at the same time as working out what you want to say.

Because we are human there will be times when we are careless listeners; listening with intent takes a lot of energy and concentration. If you are tired or overcome with emotion, for instance, you won't have the strength. These are times when our own needs naturally take over. This is only a problem when the careful listening needed to understand, enjoy, learn or help someone is happening much less than careless listening. Generally speaking, the more careful you are, the better your relationships will be. Try this exercise to assess the amount of careful/careless listening you do with the important people in your life at the moment.

*Exercise: Using a scale from 0 (none of the time) to
10 (all of the time), estimate the amount of careful
listening you do with each of the following.*

169

Intimate partner: _____
Children: _____

_____

Mother: _____
Father: _____
Brothers: _____

_____

Sisters: _____

Other Relatives: _____

_____

Best Friend: _____
Other friends: _____

_____

Boss: _____
Subordinates: _____

_____

Add any others:

Who do you listen to most carefully?   Why?

Who do you listen to least carefully?   Why?

Is there anyone with whom you would like to improve your listening?   Why?

You can take this one step further by choosing one person with whom you would like to get on better. Firstly, don't set out to do anything different but notice how you listen to them. What was your intention on each occasion? Were you listening to understand or enjoy them, to learn something or give help or comfort? If none of these, can you identify any of the reasons for not listening carefully? What were the needs you were satisfying at those times? Actually, if you did nothing else but consciously raise your awareness in this way, the quality of your listening would improve. Attentive listening would become more of a habit. However until that happens it helps to become aware of habits which we get into which block our listening. Here is a list – check whether any seem very familiar to you. Once you have identified them, it will be easier to overcome them.

Habits Which Hamper Good Listening

Measuring Constantly measuring yourself against other people makes it hard to listen because your focus is more on working out whether you are cleverer, more efficient, healthier, saner than the other person. Thoughts like, 'I would never have done that'; 'She's had things easier than me'; 'Why don't I earn as much?' use up energy that could be directed to understanding the other person.

Crystal-Gazing This is trying to read someone's mind in an attempt to find out what they are *really* thinking or feeling. You try to work out what you think they mean from subtle clues or from remembering past events. Thoughts such as 'She says she likes me, but I don't believe she means it'; 'He thinks I'm stupid, but he's too polite to actually say so'. We gaze into the crystal of our mind, focusing on our deductions, hunches, misgivings, anxieties and fears. While we are doing this, we are not listening!

Rehearsing When we are concerned about the impression we are making, we spend a lot of time thinking about what we are going to say. We rehearse in our mind while the other person is speaking and so we are only half-listening to them. It's like a game of chess; 'I'll say this, then if she says that, I'll say this, and if she says . . .'

Safety-Check In some situations we are listening to check how much of the threat to us the other person is posing. We pay attention to check whether he or she is happy or unhappy, angry or frightened. Once we've established that we're in no danger, we relax and stop listening.

Labelling Great power is carried by negative labels. It's easy to write off someone we have judged as stupid, selfish, crazy, lazy or bad in some way. It's then tempting to believe that we don't need

171

to pay too much attention to what they say. Make your judgements after you have heard everything someone has to say, rather than before they have finished.

Needing to be Right   Some of us feel very anxious if we are wrong and so we try to be right all the time. This gets us into the habit of avoiding anything which might show us up in the wrong. We twist facts, make excuses, even shout in order to prove that we haven't made a mistake. It's useful to remember that everyone makes mistakes from time to time and that, in any case, making a mistake is not the same thing as committing a sin!

Discounting   We might discount the other person in order to feel more secure ourselves. We do this in many ways. For instance instead of listening to an argument, we respond immediately by disagreeing or arguing. We might be more focused on discovering the flaws in the other person's argument than on understanding it. If you recognize this in yourself, repeat what you believe the other person's point of view to be *before* giving your own response. Try to find elements to agree with before you talk about the differences.

Sarcasm is a powerful form of discount. This is the sharp put down designed to dent the self-esteem of the other person. Janet tells her partner that the cake she baked has not been a success, only to be told, 'What did you expect? Let's face it, you'll never be Chef of the Year!'

We can discount by suddenly changing the subject or by making something into a joke.

Taking the Spotlight   This is the habit of taking everything a person says and referring it back to yourself. A friend tells you that her computer has crashed and you respond to describe the way you lost a whole chapter as the result of faulty hardware. 'It's funny you should say that, it just reminds me of . . .'; 'You think you've got problems, you should just listen to what happened to me . . .'

Finding the Answer   If someone tells us about a problem, it can

172

be very satisfying to work out a good answer and give help and advice. In fact we quite often don't even need to hear the whole story before we begin searching for the best solution. However, while we are busy working things out, we may miss hearing how the person is affected by the problem. We don't acknowledge the feelings because we don't hear them. Very often in this situation the person feels strangely alone and misunderstood; even though there is nothing wrong with the advice, this may be not what is wanted as a first response.

> *Exercise: Have you identified with any of these common habits? Having identified them, you could relate them to the earlier exercise in which you assess the amount of listening you did with important people in your life. You may find that you fall into particular habits with particular people.*

To make further use of this work, consider your pattern of listening and ask yourself the following questions having chosen one particular day – or conversation:

1   How did I usually stop myself listening?

2   How many times did I stop myself listening?

3   What actually triggered the non-listening responses I noticed?

4   When I started to respond in that way, how was I feeling?

     e.g. Bored, angry, hurt, envious, sad, excited harassed, worried, frightened, tired?

This exercise will help you understand what triggers off the behaviour that stands in the way of your listening attentively. You can take this even further by targeting one particular person and noting how you may be inhibiting your listening with them. In the next section, there are some suggestions for better quality listening. You will be able to try them out.

High Quality Listening

High quality listening is more than just keeping your mouth closed. To do it well you have to be an active participant. These are some of the skills which add up to good listening:

Mirroring   This means saying in your own words what you think someone has just said. This is probably the most important element in good listening because your mind is focused on trying to understand what the other person means, rather than on your own needs. You can start off by saying 'In other words . . .'; 'So is what you're saying . . .?'; 'You're saying you felt . . .?'; 'Do you mean . . .?'; 'What happened was . . .'

When you respond in this way the other person feels they are being heard. It is also a way of decreasing rising anger and cooling a crisis. You benefit by being able to correct misunderstandings on the spot before they escalate into communication breakdowns.

Exercise: To get practice in mirroring:

a) Ask a friend to help you and explain that you want to improve your listening skills. Ask him or her to tell you about something which has happened. Listen carefully, without interrupting, and then repeat the story back in your own words. Your friend will be able to tell you how well you have listened and understood. If you have missed anything, he or she will be able to correct you and you can have another try. Keep going until your friend is satisfied that you have understood what he or she was telling you.

b) Another way of getting practice is to record something from TV or the radio. Choose a programme where someone is talking about their personal experiences. Then practise mirroring, checking your accuracy with your tape.

174

Exploring: By adding exploring to the basic skill of mirroring you will be able to understand even more. You can ask questions for more information about the circumstances, what the person was thinking and feeling or the history leading up to the present situation. As well as clarifying things for yourself, you will be giving the other person a chance to illuminate what happened.

There are three types of questions. There are those that elicit specific information and which can often be answered with one word; e.g. 'What's the time?' 'Did you feel angry?' 'Do you approve of him?' The effect is often to shut down communication and they are often called closed questions. Once the person has answered, there is not much left to say and you either have to ask another question or change the subject.

Then there are questions to which the answer is obvious. 'Don't you think it would be a good idea to help her out?'; 'You didn't tell her everything, did you?' are examples. The questioner is leading the person to give a particular answer, rather than explore the situation. These kind of questions can be a way of covertly giving our opinion. Once again, they can close off the communication. The person has to decide whether they agree with us or not – rather than continue to explore the situation.

The most helpful type of question to ask is one which encourages the other person to continue talking. Questions like 'How did you feel about that?'; 'What did you do then?' 'What were you thinking at the time?' tend to open the door to further communication. Thus they are called open questions.

By exploring in this way you are giving the other person a clear message that you are interested in them and that you are prepared to work to know and understand them.

> *Exercise: Think of an example of a typical situation that someone might tell you about and write down how they might begin to tell you about it. Think of (a) a closed; (b) a leading and (c) an open question you could ask in response. Do this with a few different examples. If you have a friend helping you with this, you could experiment with asking the different types of question and seeing the effect of each one.*

Reaction Communication which consisted of mirroring and exploring would seem very one-sided. Having heard and understood the person you are talking with, you need to give your reactions. This means sharing your thoughts, feelings and intuition in a non-judgmental way.

You can share your perceptions or conclusions in a tentative way. 'Listening to you, I've got the idea that . . .'; 'I was wondering whether you were feeling . . .'; 'While you were talking, I began to feel . . .' The important thing is to say these things without any indication of approval or disapproval. You are genuinely checking the accuracy of your intuition.

Sharing your reactions in this way gives the other person a sense of the effect of their communication. They will also experience you as someone wanting to be together with them, rather than as someone anxious to judge them.

This kind of feedback is most helpful when it is instant, honest and supportive. Giving your reaction as soon as you fully understand the communication makes it more valuable than putting it off. Being honest about your reaction doesn't mean being rude or brutal – it means being real. Sometimes we are afraid to give our honest reaction because we fear being rejected or upsetting the other person. However, the other person will always sense we are withholding something even if they aren't clear about what it might be. The quality of the communication will always be damaged to some extent by lack of honesty.

Being honest is not the same thing as being cruel. You can be both frank and supportive. 'I'm worried that you may be missing something important' is better than 'You'd be stupid to go ahead'; 'I get the sense that there is more to this' is better than 'You're not telling me everything'. If you are nervous about giving your reaction, you could say so. 'I'm a bit nervous about telling you what I'm thinking because I'm afraid I won't be able to explain well enough.'

Using your time to listen with intent will improve the quality of your communication. You will certainly waste less time sorting out conflicts due to misunderstanding and, on a deeper level, your contact with people will feel more satisfying and rewarding.

Listening with intent means listening with empathy, openness and awareness. To be empathic means to try to understand how the other person is experiencing the world – to try to put yourself in their shoes. This is sometimes very difficult, particularly with people who behave unpleasantly; who are inconsiderate or false; who are abusive or even violent or who are very different from you. At a very basic level we are all trying to survive in the best way we can. It's not necessary to like, agree with or approve of people to understand that everyone is really engaged in the same battle. You may feel as if your listening skills desert you when you are with someone who is unresponsive to all your efforts. In such cases it is helpful to ask yourself: 'What need could this behaviour possibly be meeting for this person?'; 'What danger could this person be experiencing?'; 'What is it that this person wants from me?'

> *Exercise: Think of the last time you were with someone with whom you found it difficult to communicate because they were angry, critical, judgmental or behaving in some other defensive way. Ask the three questions above to see whether you can identify why they were behaving that way.*

This exercise is not intended to provide excuses for other people's bad behaviour. Its intention is to help you understand that behaviour.

To listen openly means listening without judging and finding fault. We've already explored how dangerous it is to prejudice a situation because we then tend to select what we hear to fit in with our judgement. The most important rule here is to hear the whole statement before you make a judgement. Mirroring, exploring and sharing your reactions are the best ways of ensuring you keep an open mind until you have enough information to work on.

When you listen to something, what you hear doesn't fall into an empty space. You have knowledge; you know about history, people, the nature of the world and so on. Listening with awareness means using this knowledge – not to make a judgement but to notice how the communication fits with the facts.

It's obvious that listening means using your ears; but your eyes are useful too. Aware listening also means noticing how body language fits in with the words. Someone can say, 'I feel fine' and at the same time be clenching their fists, tensing their shoulders, compressing their lips and generally look uncomfortable. There is a discrepancy between what they are saying and what they are doing and you can clarify and give feedback about the incongruence that you notice.

This, then, is the first of the gifts for making the best of the time you spend with people.

Gift No. 2: Expressing Yourself

Is there anything stopping you communicating your thoughts and feelings to other people? Are you holding back because you anticipate rejection or disapproval? By holding back you are protecting yourself, but you are also missing out on the feeling of closeness and equality which comes from sharing our experience with others.

Some time ago, Joseph Luft, an expert in group dynamics, came up with the idea of the Johari Window as a way of seeing how disclosure can strengthen the contact between people. His idea was to imagine your 'self' as a window with four sections:

OPEN SELF	BLIND SELF
Known to self Known to others	Unknown to self Known to others
HIDDEN SELF	UNKNOWN SELF
Known to self Unknown to others	Unknown to self Unknown to others

The first sector is your Open Self which means that it contains all your conscious actions and statements; all that is known to you and that you communicate to others. Your Blind Self consists of things that others know but of which you are unaware. All those habits, mannerisms, ways of coping that feel so natural that you no longer notice them. Your Hidden Self consists of all your secrets – thoughts, feelings, desires and experiences that you keep to yourself and that no one else knows. The fourth quarter represents your Unknown Self – unknown to you and to others. We can only guess at its existence but most people now accept that there is an unconscious part of our personality which has a large effect on us.

These are not, of course, rigid compartments. This is another way of understanding ourselves. Our thoughts and feelings, wants and needs are constantly moving from one area to another. For instance, we may expand our Hidden Self when we are with someone whom we experience as threatening; we increase our Open Self when we notice things that we pass on to others; our Blind Self is illuminated when we suddenly realize how we are affecting others.

The gift of self-expression hinges on movement of thoughts and feelings from your Hidden to your Open Self.

Exercise: Think of yourself in a few different situations or relationships. Choose a couple which you find easy and a couple you find more difficult.

Draw your own Johari's window for each one, noticing whether there is a difference in the amounts you give to each section.

Is there a situation or relationship in which you would like to be more open? Design a plan which would lead to your opening up the Blind and Hidden areas in those windows. Perhaps you could invite someone to tell you how they see you; for example you could ask how your non-verbal communication matches up with your verbal. Maybe you could choose to disclose something about yourself to another person; you might say that you find it hard to live up to your reputation as someone who is very efficient, or you could share a part of your history that you have never told anyone before.

Don't Let Fear Stop You

As you worked through the previous exercise did you feel a twinge of doubt? In theory it can seem like a very good idea to reveal yourself to others but in practice it can feel extremely risky.

For instance, the idea of self-disclosure might bring the fear of rejection, of punishment, of being gossiped about; maybe someone will laugh or be horrified. Perhaps, revealing doubts or uncertainty might lead people to lose confidence and so on. No doubt, you could make a list of the particular fears that crop up for you.

Don't ignore the fears that you identify – but don't be ruled by them. Safe self-disclosure is a matter of balance; of deciding what to tell whom. In those relationships which are important to you and in which you want the best out of the time you spend in them, the more you expand your Open Self, the better the communication will be.

Why is self-expression so important? Willingness to share our inner thoughts and feelings with people who are important to us brings several rewards.

You Will Move Closer to Others An important relationship will be deepened by the willingness of the people involved to share their inner selves. As you disclose your thoughts and feelings you come closer to each other. A relationship in which people withhold large parts of themselves will feel superficial and shallow.

You Will Learn About Yourself The whole process of clarifying your thoughts and feelings as you share them with someone increases your understanding about yourself.

You Will Improve Your Communication Skill Your willingness to disclose will encourage those you are with to do the same. The communication will deepen and feel more substantial and interesting.

You Will Lighten the Load If you are carrying a burden of cares, worries or guilt, sharing it will lighten the load. The old saying, 'A trouble shared is a trouble halved' usually turns out to be true. Telling someone about your worries doesn't, of course, solve the problems but it does relieve anxiety. You don't have to use energy to keep it to yourself and talking about it makes it possible for you to look at it more objectively. You can get useful feedback; you can examine whether your fear or guilt is justified; you can feel supported and less alone.

Exercise: This exercise is a way of assessing how much you tend to express yourself to others. It will also give you ideas on what to talk about if you want to increase how much you share of yourself with others. Across the top of a sheet of paper, write the names of the people who are most important to you: mother, father, children, partner, best friend, etc. Then down the side of the page make a list of all the things that you could talk about if you chose. Here are examples:

Likes and dislikes in foods, drinks
Likes and dislikes in music
Favourite books
Films, plays, TV programmes you have enjoyed or hated
What you think and feel about religion/politics
What you think about issues in the news
Ideas about what makes a good/bad lover, partner, parent etc.
What you enjoy/dislike about work
Your feelings about your strengths and talents
Your feelings about your weaknesses and shortcomings
Your career ambitions
How much money you earn
What you like spending your money on
Your feelings about owing or being owed money
Your feelings about your appearance
Aspects of your personality that you like/dislike
Your relationships with the opposite sex
Your relationships with people of the same sex
Your current sex life
Things in the past which you regret

Your hopes for the future
Any health problems
Any addictions which you have
Add your own ideas

Notice which categories seem easier to talk about; notice those which you rarely or never talk about. Notice whom it is you talk to and whom you hide from. Consider the decisions you are making; it is important that you don't share information in such a way that you endanger yourself. On the other hand, you may be using a log of energy hiding information which it would not be risky to share.

As a result of this exercise you may decide that you want to widen out your Open Self with some people. This exercise will help you practise. Start gently and as you gain more confidence increase the amount you choose to reveal. Always stay in control of how much you tell.

Exercise: There are three stages to expressing yourself, which allows you to stay in control of how and what you communicate. Choose a friend or acquaintance to practise with. He or she doesn't need to know that you are practising, although if it is someone whose opinion you trust you can ask them for feedback.

Stage 1:   *FACTS: Start by telling the person about something which is on your mind at the moment. Nothing too deep or emotional; perhaps something which has happened at work, your recent holiday or an interesting experience. Stick to the facts of when it happened, who was involved, what actually occurred and so on, as if you were giving a report. Don't include your own feelings or opinions at this stage.*

*If this is very new for you, don't go
any further than this until you feel
comfortable and ready to do so.*

Stage 2: *FEELINGS: Telling a story is only the
beginning of self-disclosure. The next
step is to add yourself to the story. As
well as the facts, tell the person your
thoughts and feelings; hopes and
fears; needs and wants regarding the
matter you are talking about. Stay
with topics that you feel comfortable
with until you feel ready to move to
the next step.*

Stage 3: *HERE-AND-NOW: The kind of self-
disclosure which brings you closer to
intimacy is about the thoughts and
feelings you are experiencing at this
time. For instance you can talk about
how you feel towards the person you
are with, how you feel about telling
the story, what you may be holding
back and why, what you need or want
just now. When you choose to talk in
this way you are truly bringing
yourself into the picture.*

Gift No. 3: Knowing Your Rights

This is the gift of assertion. A great deal has already been written
about assertiveness. Our particular interest in it is to learn how
an assertive approach can save you precious time. We'll begin by
clarifying what assertion actually is and what it isn't.

The assertive approach to life stems from a belief that all
people have certain rights. We are talking about basic human
rights applicable to everyone whatever their age, gender, cultural
background, physical condition, religious conviction and so on.

For instance:

• *Everyone should have the right to be treated with respect.*

This is the kind of thing that seems so obvious that it is not even worth mentioning. But we are faced every day with evidence that many people are not treated with respect. You may have faced attitudes or behaviour from other people which left you feeling disrespected and discounted. Perhaps you weren't clever enough, quick enough, pretty enough, young enough, old enough for them. An assertive person will respect themselves and others equally.

- *Everyone should have the right to express their feelings, thoughts and opinions.* You don't have the right to persuade or force others to agree with you, but you do have the right to express yourself openly and honestly.

- *Everyone should have the right to ask for what they want.* We have already worked on the importance of identifying your needs and wants. Having the right to ask for anything from anybody is not the same thing as having the right to get it! The other person also has rights which include the right to decide what to give.

> *Exercise: Having read the above examples, make your own list of basic human rights which you would like for yourself. When you have made your list, check that everything on it is something you are willing to give to everyone else. If there are some items which you would not give to everyone, take them off the list.*
>
> *Go through each item which is left and consider whether you would have to change in any way to be able to give and receive the rights you have identified.*

Assertion offers a different response to the typical fight/flight re-action described in our first chapter. To look at this in a very simple way, when we are under pressure we can go two ways. We can move into a passive or 'flight' direction or take the aggressive or 'fight' path. Assertion offers a third way, sometimes described as being in the middle of the two extremes. It is more accurate to think of it as a different approach altogether because it is a way of moving right away from either aggression or passivity. One way of understanding assertion is to compare it with aggression and passivity.

The Aggressive Approach   There is no doubt that in our society there are benefits to aggressive behaviour. In a competitive culture, aggression pays off because aggressors often get their needs met, usually at the expense of others. A truly aggressive person is very competitive and will set out to win at all costs. Such people are more likely to secure their material needs; they are able to protect themselves and take control of their lives. Every communication will carry the underlying message, 'I am more important than you and as long as you accept that there will be no problems between us.'

However, before you get too enthusiastic about the advantages – consider the penalties which are numerous:

> *Fear* If your security depends on being a winner, you are always going to be afraid of losing. Although aggressors appear to be in control, strong and confident, they often are feeling weak and vulnerable. Fear is very often at the root of aggression.
>
> *Rebellion* One way to feel safer yourself is to control other people. However, the usual result is that as people feel more controlled they will resist. They will rebel, sabotage, defy, become unco-operative and find a hundred and one ways of retaining some level of control.
>
> *Loss of Freedom* The time and energy it takes to control others means that you have much less freedom to be yourself. The paradox is that the more you try to control, the less control you actually have.
>
> *Rejection* A particularly painful result of aggressiveness is being rejected by others. Aggressive acts tend to push people away; they may submit out of fear or powerlessness but they will not want intimacy. Aggressors often feel misunderstood. They want to love and be loved like anyone else but their behaviour

185

makes it very difficult for others to treat them as equals. Other people will be defensive, nervous or competitive in their presence.

Illness As if the above wasn't enough, your good health can be corroded by aggression. The level of physical and mental tension required to maintain this reaction eventually takes its toll. Two American doctors, who were investigating the causes of heart disease identified what they called Type A and Type B behaviours. They described Type A behaviour as being observed in any person who is 'aggressively involved in a chronic, incessant struggle to achieve more and more.' Type A behaviour typically includes moving, eating, talking rapidly; impatience with the speed of progress; a high level of competitiveness; difficulty in relaxing. They found a substantial link between the Type A approach to life and heart disease.

Exercise: Think about a time when you reacted aggressively when you were under stress. Can you identify what you gained and what you lost as a result. Think about both short- and long-term gains and losses.

The Passive Approach Passivity, just like aggression, has its benefits and costs. The biggest advantage is that it allows you to keep the peace. By smoothing over differences and keeping your own desires firmly in second place, you can postpone or avoid conflict altogether. Another benefit is that other people often approve of submissive behaviour – particularly if it allows them to continue to meet their needs. If you are passive you are often not held accountable in the same way that assertive or aggressive people are. If things go wrong, it's unlikely you will get blamed because people will see you as trying to do the right thing and keeping everyone pleased. How can you be blamed if you made it clear that you were happy to go along with whatever the other person chose to do?

Another apparent advantage is that other people are often very helpful. They think the passive person is helpless, so they take over. There is another way in which the passive person benefits from their approach which may not be so obvious. Passivity can be very controlling. Think of someone you know who sulks! Sulking is a classic example of passive controlling behaviour. The sulker does nothing but the effect on others can be very destructive. The 'cry-baby' is another example. Tears are a natural expression of grief – but sometimes they can be used to control others. These are the tears which are nothing to do with grief but everything to do with getting needs met in an indirect way. It takes a hard heart to resist them!

But, just as with the aggressive approach, there is a high cost to these benefits.

> *Unmet Needs* Always trying to keep others pleased means that your own needs are unmet. A relationship based on this dynamic will tend to be less satisfying and fulfilling than one in which each person is equally sensitive to the needs and wants of the other.

> *Outbursts of Rage* There is a heavy price to be paid in repressing the anger which goes with the suppression of one's own needs. Resentment builds up and often makes itself felt in explosions of rage. 'I've spent my life helping you and what have I to show? Nothing!'; '. . . not only that, but I lent you a pencil in October 1964 and you never gave it back!!' are examples of how our own needs, even though they may not be expressed at the time, get stored up and burst out when the pressure gets too great.

> *Loss of Friendship* The liking and respect that others have for the submissive person often wanes. When someone is passive towards you, you do benefit by having your needs met, but the likelihood is that at some point you will begin to feel guilty. After a while the guilt can turn to exasperation and irritation. Resentment builds up because the relationship is so unequal and you may feel trapped by the patronage of the submissive person.

> *Helplessness* The passive response stems from a belief

that any threat or conflict is too dangerous to face; that 'flight' is the only way to survive. Passive people feel they can't initiate any action to solve a problem. Their solutions lie in appeasing or pacifying, taking the blame themselves or just keeping quiet in the hope they won't be noticed. So another cost is the constant feeling of helplessness, of being out of control of your life.

Illness Just as there is a physical cost to aggressive behaviour, passivity can also lead to problems. Emotions which are not expressed don't just disappear; it's as if the energy which the body creates as a result of our reactions gets trapped inside. This tension may well aggravate conditions like headaches, asthma, skin problems, arthritis, tiredness, anxiety states and so on.

Exercise: Think of a time when you reacted passively to a particular situation. What were your gains and losses? As in the previous exercise about reacting aggressively, think about both short- and long-term results.

The Assertive Option

Fight and flight are natural responses to threat. Assertion is a third option. One thing you might notice about assertive people is that their self-esteem is high; they are in a better position to like themselves than those who are aggressive or passive. They see themselves as essentially acceptable, even though they are not perfect. They understand that they are trying to do the best they can and when things go wrong put their energy more into finding a solution to the problem than blaming or avoiding.

Their relationships will be based on the principle of equal respect. They are willing to accord to everyone else the respect they give to themselves. People tend, therefore, to feel good in their presence. In an intimate relationship, there will be an atmosphere of acceptance and equality.

At the heart of assertion lies the ability and willingness to understand and communicate one's own and other people's needs. Clear, direct communication is the hallmark of the assertive person.

Assertion reduces fear and anxiety. If you realize that you can take the initiative in getting your needs met and stand up for yourself, you need not fear the control of others.

Bearing in mind the theme of this book, one of the greatest advantages of assertive behaviour is that you save time. Waiting for other people to guess what you want and hoping that they will give it to you can waste a lot of time. Your chances of getting what you want out of life are bound to improve as you let others know what you want. Of course, there will be times when you don't get what you want, but you will never be left with the feeling that you are completely in the control of other people. You will know that you did the best you could.

Clearly, assertion has many benefits and is a response often to be preferred to aggression or passivity. But there are costs, too.

Changing your response from either passive or aggressive may cause disruption. It may not suit other people, for instance, for you to become more willing to stand up for yourself. In an intimate relationship, any change disturbs the balance. As you become more assertive, the other person will have to adjust. If you feel threatened, they may become hostile or resentful and you may have to face the choice of returning to your old behaviour or risking the breakdown of the relationship. While some relationships will be strengthened and deepened by your developing assertions – others may break down altogether.

In order to be more assertive you might have to reappraise your own values. Say, for instance, that you have always valued strength as the most important quality; as you begin to consider the implications of respecting other people's needs and values you may find your ideas about the importance of coming out on top. If you have always valued 'peace at any price', you may come to realize that some prices are too high and choose to face the conflict. This re-examination of values is not easy and can feel quite frightening; it's like the foundations of a house being shaken and settling into another pattern. While the shaking is going on, life is not too comfortable.

How to be Assertive

Learning to be assertive doesn't mean that you must always behave that way. There will be times when it is absolutely appropriate to be aggressive, for instance if you, your family or your property are being threatened. It will also be appropriate at times to be passive; when you are being criticized by your boss, for instance. There's no point in being assertive – and redundant as a result!

No-one is consistently assertive, but you can learn assertion skills so that you can choose when and where to use them.

Exercise: Here is a way of demonstrating to yourself differences between assertive, aggressive and passive behaviour:

Passive: Imagine that you are very dependent on someone. Move your weight so that it is on one hip, put out your arms so that your hands are extended palms upright. Let your shoulders fall and your head drop down. Keeping your head bowed, look up and say in a soft voice, 'Anything you want to do is OK with me. I'll agree with anything you say. I want you to like me and I'll do anything to keep things smooth between us. I'm very sorry if I've done something to upset you and I promise never to do it again.' You can continue in this vein for as long as you want to – but as you do it, notice what happens to you. Are you physically comfortable? What kind of feelings do you have?

Aggressive: Now imagine that you know that you are right and more important than the person you are with. Stand straighter than before, but with your weight forward. With one hand on your hip and the other extended, wagging your finger. Breathe quickly and in a loud voice say, 'Who do you think you are? I've told you before things have to be done my way. I'm perfectly willing to help you but only if you appreciate the effort I'm making. You've got to realize that I know best. I'm tired of having to put your mistakes right.' Again, once you get

into the spirit you can let yourself go. Stay
aware of what happens. How do you feel? How
are you breathing? Do you feel excited? Is your
body comfortable? This may be a more enjoyable
role than the first one; even so notice whether
there is any wear and tear on your body as a
result.

Assertive: Now imagine that you are with
someone with whom you feel at ease. You are
no more and no less important. Stand with your
weight evenly distributed so that you feel solid
and secure. Straighten your spine and feel your
head free and balanced. Look straight ahead,
take a deep breath and say, 'I want to discuss
how we can work together to solve our
problems. I know that we are different but I am
sure we can work things out. I'm concerned but
I feel hopeful that we can understand each
other. I want to hear what you think and feel.'

Once again, monitor your reactions. How are
you feeling? Is this physical stance different
from the one you usually adopt? If so, do you
notice any changes in your approach as a
result?

How can assertion add to the skills of listening and self-expression? The essence of assertion is accepting that you are
intrinsically no more or less important than anyone else. Taking
this position allows you to deal with the most difficult situation
without losing your self-respect or dignity. For instance, supposing you are coming under criticism. This is one of the times when
many people find it hard to be assertive. Firstly criticism often
feels like rejection. This is one of those leftovers from childhood
when we usually felt in a 'one-down' position. After all, we were
smaller, less experienced and less knowledgeable than the criticizing parent or teacher. We assumed they were right and we
were wrong. We might have made the assumption that being
wrong was the same thing as being bad. As grown-ups we know
that human beings are not perfect and that we all make mistakes

from time to time. But somehow when we are criticized we fall back into the old habit of feeling bad and rejected.

Each one of us develops ways of minimizing the pain. Do you recognize any of these responses?

- Losing your temper and blowing up. 'How dare you talk to me like that.'

- Finding someone else to blame. 'It's nothing to do with me. Jane told me to do it.'

- Bringing up some past history in which your critic made a mistake. 'You can talk! Last year you lost a complete file.'

- Sarcasm. 'Who are you to talk! Little Miss Perfect Goodness!'

- Denying the truth. 'Who me? I wasn't even there.'

- Making the critic feel guilty. 'Well, it wouldn't have happened in the first place if you hadn't left me alone.'

These are all aggressive reactions. There are a range of passive responses:

- Silence

- Crying

- Sulking

- Pretending not to hear

- Agreeing even if you know the criticism is not true.

Some of these responses do solve the problem in the short term; the critic may be daunted by your aggression or pacified by your submissiveness. So they may seem to be the best use of your time, but in the long run they will waste time. The underlying problems will not be resolved by your aggression or passivity and so will tend to crop up again and again. Your own energy will be sapped by the need to defend yourself against the criticism.

Criticism, if it is constructive, can help you. Most of us do not want to make mistakes; if we do so it is usually due to tiredness, lack of experience or knowledge, flawed judgement of the situation or a decision to take a risk. In these cases any criticism, although it may not feel constructive, is probably accurate. Sometimes criticism you receive is not constructive or accurate – the critic has some reason of their own for judging you.

An Assertive Response to Criticism

So the first thing to do when you are facing criticism is to listen attentively and check back that you understand what the critic is saying. This will also give you time to decide whether what is being said is justified or not.

Unjustified Criticism   If you know that the criticism is unjustified and manipulative, the most effective response is to agree with it! This may seem like passivity but this strategy doesn't stem from fear of conflict; it comes from a decision not to be controlled by someone else's need to put you down.

There are four possibilities for agreement.

The grain of truth If you can find some part of what your critic is saying with which you can agree – acknowledge it and ignore the rest. For instance:

Critic: You don't really care about me. You never listen to anything I say.
You: Yes. I know that there are times when I'm impatient.
Critic: I never get to finish a sentence before you interrupt.
You: You've got a point. I know I do interrupt you sometimes.

Notice that you have kept to the truth of the situation by modifying the exaggerations. 'Never listen' becomes 'there are times'.

The probability: There may well be some chance that in

193

certain circumstances your critic might be right. For instance:

Critic: You've taken on too much. You're never going to be able to keep your deadlines.

You: You could be right. That's something I'll need to watch.

The logic: On some occasions you can agree that, although you don't agree with the premise, what the critic is saying is logical.

Critic: If you go on arguing with everything, people won't want to discuss anything with you.

You: You're right. If I were to argue with everything, people would get tired of talking to me.

The perception: Even though you may not agree at all with your critic's assessment, you could agree that it is their perception.

Critic: You're insensitive and selfish. You only ever do what you want to do.

You: I can see how you could think I was being selfish and insensitive.

The effect of this approach is usually to put the critic off balance. He or she expects you either to argue back, feel guilty or change your behaviour. However your response gives the message that you intend to take responsibility for yourself and refuse to be manipulated.

Criticism That Might Be Justified

You can't always tell right away whether the criticism is justified and intended as constructive. In that case you need to find out more. You can do this by inquiring into it before you decide whether to take it on board or not.

Focus on what you think the critic feels most strongly about and ask open questions about it. 'What is it that bothers you about . . .'; 'Is there some way in which this is upsetting you?' are examples. The questions are intended to get you information so try not to respond with questions or comments like 'What's wrong with that?' 'Don't be so picky' which will sound defensive and probably lead to an argument.

If the critic doesn't respond to your inquiry with a clear explanation of the problem then you can turn to agreeing with it in the way we explored earlier. Here is an example of how inquiry can work:

Critic:	You're so unreliable; I'm really fed up with you.
You:	What's happened to make you think that.
Critic:	I thought you were going to let me have the report by Friday. It's Monday and I'm still waiting.
You:	What is it that bothers you about waiting?
Critic:	I'm being hassled for results and I can't make a true assessment until I've got your work.

At this point you realize that the criticism is based on a real problem and is not just an attempt by the critic to make you feel bad.

Justified Criticism

When you realize that the criticism being directed at you is as a result of a problem to which you are contributing, your response needs to be a mixture of communication skills.

1. Firstly, listen and check that you have understood. Use inquiry questions if you need to get the full picture.

2. Accept responsibility for your part in the situation and express your regret.

3. Then ask questions to help you discover what changes the critic wants.

4. If you are amenable to them, make suggestions as to how these can be brought about. If you are not, check that you

understand them and share your thoughts and feelings about them.

The above scene might continue this way:

You: Am I right in thinking that you're disappointed
            that I didn't get the report to you by Friday.
Critic: Yes – I'm more than disappointed – I'm angry!
            You let me down!
You: Yes, I can see you're angry. I did give the
            impression that I would finish by Friday and I
            wasn't able to. I realize that if you were expecting
            the report it must be very frustrating for you. I'm
            sorry that I gave you a false impression. What
            would you like me to do now?
Critic: How quickly can you get it to me?
You: I am nearly finished. I reckon that if I can
            concentrate on it today, it will be ready by this
            afternoon. Would that be acceptable?
Critic: Yes – you're sure you can do it by then?
You: Pretty sure. My one worry is that if something
            else crops up that needs my attention, I'll get
            diverted. It would help if I were left alone to get
            on with this until it's finished. Could you help
            with that?
Critic: Yes – I'll tell everyone to leave you in peace.
            Thanks.

Notice that you achieved your objective – which was to stop the criticism. The conversation changed into a discussion about the best way to solve the problem. What changed it was your ability to stay assertive; communicating in such a way that you ended up with an acceptable solution to the problem.

Dealing with criticism in this way is an example of how being assertive can help you through difficult situations.

The three gifts we have explored so far are designed to increase the quality of your relationships. The next two are useful when problems occur.

11

WHEN THINGS GO WRONG

Have you spent time lately:

- dealing with the fall-out from conflict with someone close to you?

- arguing with someone you are close to without coming to any agreement?

- beating around the bush in order to avoid conflict?

- feeling depressed or angry about an unresolved disagreement?

- deliberately not speaking your mind or asking for what you want because you don't want to fight?

Time spent like this is often time wasted because the conflict does not get resolved and keeps cropping up in different ways. The fourth gift of meeting conflict comes into its own in situations like this.

Gift No. 4: The Skills of Meeting Conflict

Melanie has been teaching all day. She loves her job but she has a difficult class and today has been particularly demanding. She is looking forward to a quiet evening at home unwinding and relaxing with her partner, Derek.

Derek, an up-and-coming businessman, has invited some representatives from another company who are showing interest in his product home for dinner. He is a great believer in using social occasions to oil the wheels of business negotiation. He is excited about the prospects for the future. He and Melanie want to buy a house and start a family, and he feels that this deal will help them on the way.

They arrive home:

Derek: Hi, how was your day?

Melanie: Well, Class 111 were hell today – but I'm getting somewhere with Joe – he was really trying to be co-operative. How about you?

Derek: I've got fantastic news! You remember McGregor and Donald? Well they're interested – and I've asked them over this evening for dinner.

Melanie: What? You must be joking!

Derek: I think they're ready to buy. This evening could clinch it. I'll help with the meal – we'll keep it simple.

Melanie: That's not the point. I'm tired. I don't want to make pleasant conversation to people I don't even know.

Derek: But it's all fixed! They'll be here at eight.

Melanie: I'm not doing it. You haven't considered me at all.

Derek: But I'm doing all this for you. This deal will make all the difference. You're so selfish – you never want to put yourself out to help me!

Melanie: How can you say that! I'm the one who never gets considered!

It's not difficult to imagine how the scene continues. They prepare the meal with bad grace, banging around the kitchen. The visitors enter an atmosphere of charged feelings. Melanie and Derek manage the evening with brittle conversation and overdo the politeness to each other. The visitors leave, confused and slightly uncomfortable. Melanie and Derek clear up in silence and then go to bed, still not speaking to each other.

It is inevitable that conflicts will arise from time to time in relationships. Being able and willing to meet and face the conflict is much healthier than avoiding it. Keeping your anger under wraps has the effect of clogging up the communication channels.

A relationship in which you can express your anger and negotiate together is likely to develop into a powerful and strong closeness. You will know more about yourself and each other; you will be able to acknowledge your own and each other's feelings without being afraid of them; you will have greater freedom to be yourself without needing to keep up the masks which hide your true feelings.

Healthy fighting is a way of expressing anger so that you don't just offload your feelings or bottle them up so that they burst out when the pressure becomes too great.

The Best Time In most situations the best time is the present. Putting a conflict off nearly always loses more time than it saves. For one thing, your thoughts and feelings about the situation have a way of intruding into whatever you are doing instead so that your concentration and effectiveness are affected. Also, a conflict has a way of making itself felt even if it is being avoided or covered up. Tempers get short, feelings run high, accidents happen, innocent people get shouted at and so on. Confronting a problem the moment it emerges is the best way to stop it growing into a major crisis. You can stop what you are doing and make time then and there to sort out what's happening. If you do it's important to mark what you are doing. You might say, 'Look, we've got a problem about this – let's stop what we're doing and see if we can deal with it before it gets too difficult.' If this isn't practical, schedule a time, preferably within the next 24 hours. Actually deciding on a time has the effect of cooling things down for the moment and focuses the attention of everyone involved on what is happening.

Check Your Motives Before you engage in any important conflict, give yourself a quiz. Ask youself, 'Why do I want to do this? What do I want to achieve? What is it that is annoying me? What is he/she actually doing or not doing? What do I want him/her to do differently? Is what I want reasonable? Is what I'm feeling reasonable? and so on.

What is the Problem? When you finally get together to have the discussion, having set a time and clarified your thinking, start by describing how you see the problem. Keeping it clear and

199

THE TIME OF YOUR LIFE

simple, tell the other person what he or she does or doesn't do. Stick to the facts without blaming or being personal. If you think you would find this difficult, write it out beforehand or practise saying what you want. You could begin by saying, 'There's something I would like to talk about. It's important to me and I've been thinking about it for some time. When you interrupt me before I get to the end of what I want to say ...' or 'I notice that you haven't done your turn at the washing up this week ...'

An important element in how you begin is that you talk specifically about *behaviour* and not *personality*. It is tempting to say things like, 'You're so lazy/rude/unhelpful/selfish/uncaring/ ...' but if you do, you are bound to make things worse. We tend to defend ourselves against personal attacks – and if the person you are with gets defensive, you will not be able to have a reasonable discussion. If you see that the person is reacting defensively, backtrack by saying something like 'I can see this is hurtful, but you're reacting as if I'm making a personal attack on you. I'm not, I'm only talking about something you do – not what you are.'

How Does It Affect You? The second thing to talk about is the effect on you. Use 'I' statements to describe how you feel – angry, hurt, disappointed, and so on. 'When you interrupt me before I finish the sentence, I feel angry and think that you don't consider what I say is important' or 'I notice that you haven't taken your turn at washing up and I feel disappointed that the agreement we made isn't working. Make it clear that you are taking responsibility for how you think and feel and not blaming the other person.

What Do You Want? Keep in mind the assertion principle that you have a right to ask for what you want. State clearly, simply and directly what changes you want the other person to make. Be specific and talk in terms of behaviour rather than attitude. 'I would like you to wait till I finish what I'm saying' is better than 'I want you to be more considerate'; 'I'd like you to do the washing up now' is better than 'You should take your turn'. Remember that you are making a request – not a demand.

What Do You Hope For? Tell the other person the benefits of their agreeing to change. Talk about any material benefits like better controlled finances, more space, more equally shared chores and so on. There might also be emotional gains like less stress, a better feeling, fewer arguments etc. You can also talk about what you will do if the change doesn't come about – but you need to be careful here. Don't make threats you are not prepared to carry out and be careful not to over-dramatize the situation. 'I'll never speak to you again!'/'I'll leave you' may sound as if they are strong bargaining points but you are weakening your position by such threats unless you actually mean them.

What is the Response? Now it's time for you to put your listening skills to the test. Let the other person respond and use your listening skills to check that you understand the response you are getting.

The other person will either:

- Agree with your view of the situation and fall in with what you want.

- Agree to what you want with some conditions.

- Agree to some of what you want.

- Refuse to co-operate, perhaps with hostility.

- Refuse what you want, but suggest a 'trade'. 'I won't do this, but I'll do that'.

- Ask for time to consider.

How Will It End?

Check that you understand what the other person is prepared to do. If you have an agreement you can declare the conflict over. It is wise to set a trial period so that you can review how things are going. If you haven't been able to come to an agreement, restate what you think the position is: 'I've explained how I feel about things and said as clearly as I can what I would like to happen. I understand that you don't agree with me. Do you have a solution?'/'Well, at least we've cleared the air between us even though we don't agree on what to do next. Let's talk about this again,' are examples of how you can keep the door open. The fact that you haven't been able to sort things out this time need not stop you.

Make a date for the next round so that you can continue to work for change.

Here is an example showing how Melanie used these ideas to face her conflict with Derek.

Her motives Melanie was very angry at Derek for the way in which he had asked the visitors to dinner. On quizzing herself she realized that some of her anger was about her feeling of being taken for granted by Derek and some was left over from her frustration with the children she had been teaching that day. She had felt discounted when Derek had ignored what she had said about her difficulties at school.

The time

Melanie: I want to talk about what happened yesterday evening. Can we make some time after dinner?

Derek: Yes, OK.

The problem

Melanie: There are two things that I want to discuss. When you arrived home and said you had invited McGregor and Donald to dinner (*behaviour*) . . .

The effect

. . . I felt very angry. I was tired and really just wanted to rest. I was also upset because you didn't seem to care about the difficulties I was having at school . . . When you asked me what kind of day I had, you didn't respond at all to what I said (*behaviour*) and I felt very discounted (*effect*).

The desired change

. . . I would have preferred it if you had phoned me during the day to check what I wanted; or asked them later in the week. I'd also like to talk about how I'm

202

experiencing School at the moment because I feel very stressed by how things are going.

The hope

... If you do call me in advance, I won't feel so resentful at being taken for granted. If we can talk about how things are going for me at work I'll have a chance to explore what's happening and whether I could be dealing with things in a different way.

The response

Melanie: I've said how I see things; what do you feel about it?

Derek: I realized that things were going wrong during the evening, but I didn't realize that I had ignored you. I was very excited about what was happening, and I can see how I just missed your reaction. I think you're right, it was unreasonable and I'm sorry you ended up feeling so upset ...

The negotiation

... I will try to remember to contact you before I make any arrangements, but it might not be always possible. If I can't contact you, we'll go out to a restaurant so that you won't have to make any preparations. Do you think that would work?

Melanie: OK. Yes I'd be willing to do that – unless I'm very tired. I would like to feel that I could opt out if I really don't want to go out.

Derek: That's reasonable – though these things always seem to go better if you're there. But I can understand that you don't always feel like it.

Melanie: Right. Let's agree that we'll discuss whether to have people home in the evening and that if you can't get hold of me, you'll arrange for a restaurant dinner. I will make an effort to come but I'm free to say 'no' if I really am too tired.

Derek: Yes, I agree to that. Now, tell me about how
              things are at School . . .

Both Melanie and Derek clearly want to resolve the conflict and
they are willing to use their skills to that end. They avoid getting
defensive and use their time and energy to try to understand and
negotiate.

> *Exercise: Play back in your mind a time when you
> have been in conflict with someone. Choose a time
> when things did not go well for you. Write out
> what happened as if it were a scene in a play. Now
> compare what you have written with the ideas in
> this section and rewrite the script as it might go if
> you were to follow the guidelines.*

These guidelines will help you to meet and manage conflict:

- *Treat the other person with respect:* Respect is conveyed by
  your tone of voice, how you listen, the gestures you make,
  the language you use. Disagreeing with another's beliefs,
  values or priority of needs does not mean that you can disrespect the person. Disrespect is shown by sarcasm, verbal
  attack, put-downs, overlooking needs, disregarding points of
  view, dismissive body language and so on.

- *See things from the other side:* We have already explored the
  concept of attentive listening. Listening in this way means
  you can more easily empathize with the position of the other
  person. Empathizing means trying to see the world as the
  other sees it – it isn't enough to say, 'I know just how you
  feel.' Even if you have had the same experiences as each
  other, your perception may be very different.

- *Don't hit below the belt:* We accept that everyone has their
  tolerance level for physical pain and hitting below the belt is
  seen as unfair. We also have our emotional vulnerabilities;
  we can take a certain amount of pain but once that point is
  reached we have to defend ourselves. If you say something
  'below-the-belt' to someone you are fighting with, he or she

will not be able to respond rationally. They will be more aware of the pain they are feeling than anything else. Just as with physical pain, people can differ in how much they can take so you need to be aware of the tolerance level of the person you are with.

- *Keep to eight-year-old language:* Managing conflict in this way does mean talking about your inner thoughts and feelings; needs and wants. Keeping your language direct and simple will help your message get across without misunderstanding. If you find yourself getting tied up in knots, think how an intelligent eight-year-old would express what you are feeling. This usually helps you to cut through the verbiage which may be concealing the truth of what you want to say.

- *Stay in the present:* Don't confuse the current issue by introducing history. It is tempting in the heat of the moment to bring in all the old hurts and grievances but doing so will only weaken your present position. Deal with what is happening now because you cannot change anything that happened in the past. If you do have a large collection of unspoken complaints, it's a sign that you haven't been managing conflict very well up to now. Let them go and make a resolution not to create another collection.

- *Avoid sneaky power-plays:* Sometimes you or the other person gets tempted into trying to sneak an agreement by:

  attacking the person: 'You are too inexperienced to know anything about this'/'You're ignorant'

  trying to shame the person: 'How could you say a thing like that?'/'I would never have expected that from you'

  appealing to morality: 'I thought you were a responsible person'

  bribery: 'I'll pay you if you help me'/'I'll love you if you do as I say'

  control: Shouting, overtalking, sulking and so on.

All of these are to be avoided because you will never get a wise, long-lasting agreement from them.

- *Be willing to give and take:* Much of the emphasis of this section has been on how you can communicate your perception and ask for what you want. It is just as important to take this from your partner assuming that he or she also has discontents. Be willing to listen to the other side, using all the listening skills we have already explored: reflecting, paraphrasing, giving feedback and so on.

Letting Off Steam

There are bound to be times when you are so uptight with irritation or frustration that you know you are not in a good state to conduct these very rational and reasonable sessions. Here are a couple of ways of managing this situation.

Opening the Box   Both parties need to have agreed the rules for this in advance. The structure allows you to air your feelings without fear of any counterblows.

1 Set a time limit: 'I want to open the box for two minutes about . . .' The other person can negotiate for less time or make a time in the future or refuse to have the box opened.

2 Open the box: 'I'm angry about . . .' Go on for exactly the time you agreed, talking clearly and directly and giving vent to your thoughts and feelings. The rule for your partner is that he or she will not interrupt, offer explanations or become defensive.

3 Finish: When the time is up, stop. Your partner says, 'I heard you; thank you.'

4 Let it go: The agreement is that neither partner will say anything about the topic for at least an hour. After that time, if either party wants to take it up, you can use the conflict management ideas already discussed.

The Explosion

There are times when you get angry but can't express it at the time or to the people involved. Perhaps other people aren't even involved, you may be angry at an organization, a system or the world in general! 'The Explosion' enables you to get it off your chest. When you find yourself full of anger and frustration that has nothing to do with your partner, you can tell him or her that you are going to explode! Let your partner know that it isn't personal but that you just need an audience.

When you have had your say, ask your partner for anything that will make you feel better – a hug, a cup of tea, advice, silence or whatever you need at the time.

Allow your partner, too, to explode whenever it seems necessary. Don't take it personally and be ready with whatever support is asked for.

Gift No. 5: Negotiating So That Everyone Wins

Have you ever:

- Asked for a rise in wages?

- Disputed a mark given by a teacher?

- Asked for compensation for something you were not satisfied with?

- Applied for a job?

- Bought or sold a house?

- Sued someone?

Any time there is a gap between what you want and what you've got you are faced with the problem of closing the distance. The problem may involve other people with whom you are not intimate enough to use the strategies of conflict resolution of self-expression already described. We have reached the fifth goal – negotiation skills. These are skills which help you come to a fair agreement with people who may have very different needs from your own.

Even the most complicated situation can be broken down into stages:

Stage 1: Attend To Any 'People' Problem When you are dealing with someone who is preventing you getting what you want you can easily forget that you are with a person. Somehow the person gets to be perceived as 'the other side', 'the enemy' or 'the problem'. When this happens, communication can break down altogether.

Imagine the scene between a teenager, Beatrice and her mother, Margaret. Beatrice has asked her mother if she can go to a party given by one of her friends.

Margaret: What time will it finish?
Beatrice: I don't know! You always put a damper on what I want to do.
Margaret: I haven't done any such thing. I think it's reasonable to ask when it ends. I don't want you out late at night.
Beatrice: Don't you trust me to look after myself?
Margaret: Yes, but . . .
Beatrice: You never let me do anything. Everyone else is going.
Margaret: You're looking for a fight. I just asked when it ended but if you can't even tell me that then I'm not going to consider you going at all.
Beatrice: I hate you . . . *slammed door.*

By now each sees the other as unreasonable and part of the problem which has become how to persuade the other.

Beatrice saw her mother's question as wanting to stop her fun rather than as an expression of concern. Margaret saw Beatrice's reaction as an effort to control her mother rather than get her own needs met.

So now there are two levels to their problem. One is the obvious one of how to negotiate whether Beatrice attends the party and what time she comes home. The other is less obvious and hinges on the nature of their relationship. There is often a tension between teenagers and their parents which arises from the process of separation. The teenager is becoming more dependent and the parent is faced with the task of helping them to negotiate the tricky road to adult maturity.

Most negotiators have these two interests at heart – they want to achieve the 'task' of fulfilling their own needs – whilst maintaining the relationship with the other side. When a negotiation becomes a contest, the nature of the relationship can get tangled up with the problem and cause a great deal of confusion as well as wasting a lot of time.

If this happens, it is vital to separate the relationship from the 'task'. Dealing with the problem and the relationship need not be conflicting goals. If you think that one of the things holding up a reasonable agreement is the nature of the relationship – deal with that first. Here are some basic principles to follow:

- *Understand your opponent's thinking:* When there is a serious disagreement each side tends to see only the merits in their case and the faults in the other person's. Your ability and willingness to see the situation as the other sees it is an important skill which will help you communicate effectively. Beatrice's thinking is influenced by her need to feel part of the crowd; Margaret is concerned with the potential dangers of late-night parties. Each of them is 'right' in terms of their own needs yet each believes the other to be 'wrong'.

- *Understand your own reactions:* If you have a strong reaction against the person with whom you are negotiating, check where this reaction stems from. Is there, for instance, some way in which this person reminds you of someone else in your life whom you disliked or distrusted? Does their tone of voice, their appearance, the gestures they use evoke memories in you? Are you responding more to these memories from the past than to what is happening in the present?

- *Give a reward:* Understanding how your opponent is thinking will enable you to make suggestions which they are able to accept without losing face, feeling put down or bypassed. No one likes to lose and very often people will resist a practical and wise solution because it will seem like backing down if they agree. Search for a solution which has a reward in it for the other person.

- *Don't waste time blaming:* Finding a way to blame the other person for the problem may give you a fleeting feeling of self-justification but it will not solve the problem. Blaming is rarely productive. Even if you are right, once you attack the other person they will become defensive and you will have gained little.

- *Acknowledge feelings:* When you are involved in a negotiation check how you are feeling. Are you angry, frustrated or scared? Is your breathing speeding up? Are you finding it difficult to stay relaxed? Watch and listen to the other person – how do you think he or she is feeling? Notice, for instance, whether anything in particular seems to raise their anxiety. Get into the habit of asking yourself, 'What could be causing their anger/anxiety?' 'Is it possible that something from the past is intruding?' 'Is there a personal problem which is affecting him/her?' 'Why am I feeling the way I do? Am I responding to my feelings towards him/her rather than trying to find a solution?' and so on.

  Talk about feelings, your own and the other person's. Saying something like, 'You know, I'm feeling angry about the situation. I feel I have been treated unfairly and I'm worried that we won't be able to come to an agreement. I can see that you are also not happy with how things are', certainly won't harm you. You will seem more like a 'real person' and the other person may be more open with you.

- *Allow letting off steam:* It is hard to think clearly when you are in the grip of strong feelings which you can't express. By acknowledging feelings and encouraging their expression you can clear the way for a rational discussion. People do experience release from tension by being able to state their grievances. Allow the other person to talk about their feelings without interruption. Encourage them to continue until they have run out of things to say. Listen quietly, don't repond other than to check whether there is anything else the person wants to say.

In the kind of situation we are now exploring, it is even more important that you use your communication and listening skills to the best advantage.

- *Listen attentively* and reflect what is being said. The discipline of always reflecting back what you have heard before you give your response will help you understand the other's perceptions and feelings, as well as giving you time to frame your response. If you pay attention and say 'I just want to check that I understand what you are saying . . .' the other side will understand that you are serious about communicating. They will also feel heard and understood. It is difficult to treat someone who is trying hard to understand you as an enemy.

- *Summarizing* is another skill which is very helpful. From time to time you can say, 'Let's just see where we've got to. You've said that . . . and I've replied . . .; we've covered the following options . . . Is that how you see our position at the moment?' If an argument becomes heated it is easy to get stuck in arguing details so that you lose sight of the wood for the trees. Summarizing has the effect of giving pause to the argument which may be getting heated. It also lays out the situation so that you can see both the wood *and* the trees.

- *Speak for yourself, not for the other person.* Criticizing the other person is rarely helpful. If you say something that is felt to be untrue or unfair, you will be ignored or fought against. The other person will put all their energy into proving you wrong rather than finding a good solution. 'I feel let down' is better than 'You betrayed me'; 'I feel oppressed' is better than 'You're a racist'.

- *Speak sparingly* especially if feelings are running high. It's easy to say too much. Think before you speak and if in doubt, keep your mouth shut! If you are finding it difficult to contain yourself but realise that you might regret saying what's in your mind – ask for a break so that you have time to check what you want to say and why. In any case, a break is often a good idea if you feel locked in a disagreement.

- *Create a working relationship:* If the personal relationship

211

between you is bad, accept it and create a working relationship. You don't have to like someone to be able to work for an acceptable agreement. You could say, 'Look, I know that we don't get on because our views are so different but we do need to get together to try to sort out this problem. Let's try to put our personal feelings aside. How do you see the situation? . . .'

Stage 2: Needs Before Solutions Problems eat up time and we can easily get tempted into thinking only about the best solutions. Strangely enough, although this may seem the best way to save time – it wastes time in the end. The best preparation for a win/win result is to think about the problem in terms of the *needs* rather than *solutions*.

Here is an example of the difference this can make:

A staff group is meeting in a stuffy room. Sally suggests opening a window because the airless atmosphere is making it difficult to concentrate. Judy immediately disagrees, saying she has a cold and doesn't want to sit in a draught. On the face of it there doesn't seem any way of meeting both needs – they are in direct conflict. But look at this in terms of needs. If Sally restates her solution in terms of need she might say, 'I need to have more fresh air.' Judy would say, 'I need to stay out of draughts.' Now other options can be considered – like opening a window in an adjoining room; Judy moving so that she is not next to the window; having a break to get fresh air outside the room; and so on. If the group only discusses whether or not to open the window, whatever they decide Sally and Judy either win or lose. As the group discusses how to meet both people's *needs*, both of them can win and conflict is avoided.

> *Exercise: Think of a conflict situation from the past or present for which you have not been able to find a solution. Write down the names of the people involved and under each name jot down the needs which you think that each person is trying to meet.*

Identifying needs means being able to distinguish between *means*

212

and *ends*. A form of words which will help you clarify your needs is 'I need ... because ...' What comes after the 'because' is the most important part of the sentence.

Sometimes the conflict of needs is obvious. You may need your money back for a faulty article; the shop assistant may have been instructed to give credit not cash. You may need the car to get to your meeting; your partner has another meeting in the opposite direction. You may need peace and quiet; your neighbour may have four noisy dogs and several children.

On the other hand, conflict often brings stress. Stress makes it difficult to think and analyse a situation clearly. Someone who wants to avoid conflict may disguise their needs by using indirect language. Maybe only their body language is expressing what they are wanting. Stress also makes it difficult to listen attentively. As a result it can take a long time to uncover the needs which lie behind the conflict.

To help you clarify the needs which lie behind a particular position get into the habit of asking 'Why' or 'Why not?' Asking yourself these questions may help you clarify what the other is hoping for. You can also ask the other person why they are taking a particular position. Be careful that you ask in such a way as to make it clear that you are not asking the person to justify themselves, but to help you understand their needs and wants, hopes and fears. 'What are your main worries about ...?'/'What do you see as the benefits of ...?' are possible ways of finding out what lies behind their stand.

Asking yourself 'Why not?' is also a good way of uncovering interests. After all you have good reasons for holding your view – why is it that the other person sees things differently?

One other consideration is the larger picture of interests. Even in the simplest two-sided negotiation, each person is probably serving several interests. Our parents, children, partners, business colleagues, friends and so on may have expectations of us to which we are sensitive. Sometimes it's helpful to wonder whether there are any invisible presences sharing the room. For instance, appearing to back down will be very difficult for someone who is being pressured by a boss to appear strong.

Stage 3: Where Are Your Meeting Points: Although the differences between you may be clear, there are probably some things you agree on. Suppose the argument is about whether to go on holiday to the seaside or a town. Each person has their reasons for their particular position, but each would probably agree that holidays are a good thing. Identifying and discussing those things on which you agree creates a feeling of mutuality and moves you away from digging into opposing positions.

If you can't find any meeting point at all, you need to say something which shows you are respectful of the person you are negotiating with even though you cannot find anything with which to agree in their position.

One of the shared interests between Beatrice and Margaret is that they both want to manage the development of an interdependent rather than a dependent relationship between them. What they are arguing about are the details of how this can best be achieved.

Stage 4: Work Out How Everyone Can Win By now you will have stated your views, listened to the other side, identified needs and discussed any shared interests. The next stage is to try to generate ideas which give all sides something of what they want.

Margaret might be willing to allow Beatrice to go to the party if she is willing to be home by an agreed time; or she might suggest having a party at their house so that she can meet Beatrice's friends; or she can arrange to collect Beatrice. Once they move away from trying to control each other, they may well come to an agreement which helps Beatrice towards independence and Margaret to begin to loosen the ties of parenthood.

A useful method to employ is brainstorming (described in Chapter 4). Briefly, brainstorming means:

1 Generating as many ideas as possible in a short amount of time.

2 No evaluation or critical judgement of ideas at this stage.

3 The zanier the better; allow any notion regardless of practicality.

4 Try to top each other's ideas; one of you may come up with an incomplete idea that triggers thoughts for the other.

5 List *every* idea.

6 Discuss each option only when the process is complete.

In inventing options, avoid searching for a single answer. Work from the assumption that you are both right and that there is a way to satisfy each of you – rather than from the assumption that only one of you is right.

Stage 5: Make a Proposal   At this stage give yourself and your opponent time to consider the various options and decide which ones you like best. As you talk, offer choice and invite discussion. Avoid giving an ultimatum. If you sense that your opponent is prepared to accept one of your options, make a suggestion that they would find it possible to accept. How you word your proposal is important. Try to make it a question that the person cannot answer with a refusal. For example, 'If I say "yes" to the party, would you be willing to be home by midnight?' is better than, 'I'll only let you go if you are home by midnight.' 'If I make the preparations, would you be able to get the meal ready tonight.' is better than, 'I want you to get the dinner ready tonight.' 'Would you rather do the washing up now or after the TV programme' is better than 'I want the washing up done.'

Stage 6: Don't Forget the Details   When you have an agreement, spend some time working out the details. Who is going to do what, when and for how long? Don't let your elation at reaching an agreement stop you working out the nitty gritty details. It is helpful to make a date to get together to check how things are going. It's a good idea to write down agreements, so that in future there can be no confusion as to what was actually fixed.

If It Doesn't Work: If it looks as if you are not going to succeed on this occasion check that you haven't:
Ignored the feelings: Remember that when feelings are running high, they have to be dealt with or they will inhibit progress.
Forgotten to listen: In the heat of the moment, it is possible that you haven't listened long or attentively, acceptingly or empathetically enough to understand the other person's need.
Judged options too soon: If you got as far as brainstorming, you

may have stopped the process by evaluating the options before the process was finished.

Missed out the details: You may have felt awkward about working out the details once an agreement was reached. It seems to some people that it is a sign of distrust – and yet not to do so may lead to failure. Either the other person didn't really feel committed to making it work or didn't really know how to. Either way there is no way to hold someone to account if the details were never agreed.

The fault may not lie with you. Some opponents have more power than you and use it. In this kind of situation you have to be realistic. Before starting the negotiation, figure out what you will do if you get turned down. If for instance you are negotiating for a higher wage and know that if you don't get it, you will leave for the job offer you received yesterday, you are in a good position. On the other hand, if you can't fall back on a job offer and know that your best alternative is to continue in the present job drawing whatever salary is offered, your position is not so strong.

Whatever your alternative, do your homework. Check that any facts and figures you are using to support your case are accurate. If at all possible, use objective criteria to assess your situation. For instance, you can quote salary scales which already exist, or research which supports your case. Then appeal to the person's sense of justice and hope for the best.

Maybe things have ground to a halt because the other person has dug in their position and refuses to budge. If this happens, resist making an all-out attack on the person. Try to look behind their position for the reasons. Ask questions and listen to the answers.

There are any number of ploys that people can use to avoid negotiating – lying, deceiving, bribing, manipulating, shouting, refusing to speak, attacking you personally and so on. The best tactic to handle this kind of thing is to stop talking about the problem and insist on talking about what is happening between you. For example, 'I find it very difficult to continue because you are shouting at me. I'm guessing that's because you are angry – let's stop so that you can tell me what you are angry about.'

This process for working through a situation where negotiation is necesary has many applications. You can employ it at home, school or at work. You can use it if you want to set goals for change which will mean that other people have to change in some way. It is a good way of ensuring that time is used to the best advantage.

Take Your Time: These five gifts or talents are well within your reach, even if you did not have a good fairy to give them to you at birth. Working through the book will have prepared you well for taking control of your time. The next chapter is the last and offers you the opportunity to consider how the circle of your life will be completed.

12

THE BIRD IS ON THE WING

The Bird of Time has but a little way
To fly – and Lo! the Bird is on the Wing.

Edward Fitzgerald (1809-93) The Rubaiyat of Omar Khayam

The theme of this book has been the management of time. We
have explored the subject from many angles: how your early experiences influence the way that you are using time now; how to
assess how well you are doing at the moment; practical ways of
making changes so that you feel more satisfied with how things
are going; how to deal with some of the problems that get in the
way.

By now you should have lots of ideas about how to manage time
effectively. You will also be clearer about what you want to
achieve in the time you have. This last chapter is about the end of
the process and about how you can be in charge of that as well as
all the rest.

The advances in sanitation, nutrition and disease control of
this century mean that people can expect to live into a ripe old
age; maybe up to ten, twenty or even thirty years after retirement
from work. This can be a wonderful gift of time in which, with
good health, good friends and sufficient income we can explore
aspects of ourselves and our life as we may not have had time to
do before. Time, for instance, to think, to travel, to learn a language, to paint, to read and so on.

How do you feel about ageing? Do you search the mirror each
morning for the signs? Are you looking forward to being a senior

citizen? Generally speaking our culture does not encourage positive thinking about becoming older. Whereas in some societies, age brings with it automatic respect and the assumption of wisdom, in our predominantly white, Western culture we tend to stave it off as long as possible. Old people are frequently pushed aside by the ambitious young; old-age homes are all too often dreary places. The spirit of this book is about taking control and managing the time of your life as well as possible. You don't have to give up this control when you move into the last decades.

If you have worked through the goal-setting exercises, check over them to see how you are planning for your old age. Is there anything you need to be doing now to ensure that you have as many resources as possible later in your life? Don't only think about material resources – are you mentally and spiritually prepared?

> *Exercise: When you were a child, who was the oldest person you knew? How was he or she treated by the family? What kind of a life did he or she live? Was it an active, exciting lifestyle? Was there very little contact with people? 'Was the person ill? Were they happy or miserable? What was your feeling towards them?*
>
> *Have these feelings in any way affected how you feel about your own old age?*

The Completion of the Circle

All cultures seem to have their taboos – facets of life which are not to be spoken about openly. In some societies it might be sexual matters that are kept private, in others money. For many people living in this British society death comes into that category. What was your own reaction when you realized the subject of this chapter? Were you intrigued? Interested? Shocked? Embarrassed? Does it seem morbid? Have you decided not to read much further? It is rare to talk about death – particularly your own. When someone close to us dies, we grieve in a very personal way with little public display.

There are different attitudes towards death; for some it is a continuation of life, simply in a different form. Death can be accepted as a natural part of life. Elizabeth Kubler-Ross who has written a great deal about this subject called it 'the final stage of growth'. For others death is the end of everything and something to be resisted and feared.

Exercise: Find a time and space where you can be on your own for a while. Sit comfortably and relax. Can you remember when you first became aware of death? Perhaps you had a pet that died. Maybe an aged relative passed away.

How did your parents and the other adults around you respond? Did they talk to you about what had happened? Did they change the subject? Did they hide their feelings from you?

How did you feel about what happened? How do you feel now in thinking about it?

Is there any connection between those events and your present thoughts and feelings about death?

Our first experience of death is likely to influence how we perceive the whole subject. Parents, usually from the best of intentions, want to protect their children from the pain of the death of a loved person. So they hide their feelings and try hard to distract the child from thinking sad thoughts. Under these circumstances it is difficult to work out how to think or feel about death. If the grown-ups are frightened, it's logical for the child to think that death is bad and fearsome.

Exercise: Take a sheet of drawing paper and some paint or coloured pens or pencils. Give yourself a moment to relax and then draw an image to represent your idea of death. If you don't know how to start this, just put the brush or pen on the paper and start doodling, playing with the shapes and colours.

When you have finished, look over the image that you have created. Does it have anything to tell you about your attitude to death?

The way you approached this exercise could be significant. Which colours did you choose, for instance? Some people draw in dark colours with thick lines; others use light, bright shades. Similarly, the different ways of symbolizing death can range from a staircase leading to a bright light in the sky to a cloaked, sinister and shadowy figure.

Death is not something that most people consciously think about a great deal but there are times when the problems brought to a counsellor have fear or denial of death at their root. Denise, who talked about her fear of travelling too far away from home; Bernie who seemed to have everything life could offer but felt generally anxious and unhappy; Sharon who lived her life at a frenetic pace cramming more into a day than most people do in a week; Andrew who wouldn't commit himself to any permanent relationship because of his fear of being abandoned. As each talked about their thoughts and feelings and what they wanted out of life, they revealed fears about their own inevitable deaths or those of people close to them. As they faced and accepted the inevitability of the end, it seemed more possible for them to take control over the nature of their living. It is as if the energy which had been used in protecting themselves from the idea of death was freed up for living.

Exercise: Once again, finding a time and space where you will be uninterrupted for a while, sit comfortably and relax.

Imagine yourself waking up on the morning of what will be the last day of your life. How old are you? Are you in good health or in a sick bed? Are you alone? If not, who is with you?

Imagine yourself living this last day. What do you say and do?

How does the moment of death come? Is it accidental? The result of a risk you have taken? A gentle slipping away? Do you imagine yourself dying in the same manner as someone else you know or knew?

When you have finished this exercise, write or draw the story of your death as you thought and felt it.

Remind yourself that this was a daydream you created and that you don't have to turn the dream into reality. However this is an important exercise because it will help you to be aware of unconscious fantasies you may have about any script you may have developed about the time and manner of your death. Once aware, you can create a new script if the one you have is not what you wish.

Ben came into counselling at the age of forty-five. He was overweight and smoked heavily. He was very successful at the business he ran but had begun to feel depressed – that 'life was not worth living' – for no apparent reason. As he and the counsellor explored what was happening, Ben realized that he was certain that he would die at about the same age as his father who had a heart-attack when he was fifty. As he uncovered this unconscious belief, he also realized that he could change his script into one of long life rather than life cut short. He lost weight and stopped smoking! He began to feel that life was worth living after all. He is now fifty-five and healthy. Of course, he might die suddenly of a heart-attack – writing a new psychological script is not a magic cure or a guarantee of long life! But the time he is living now is no longer dogged by feelings of depression and hopelessness.

Exercise: Returning to the previous exercise, look at what you have written or drawn. What does this tell you about the way your life is 'scripted' to end? Are you happy with this? How would you like to change it?

If there are changes you want to make, write a new script for that last day.

The fears people have about death are varied. Some are afraid they will suffer a long and painful illness; some that they will be old and abandoned; others that they will die before they can achieve their lifetime goals. For many people the fear is about the finality of the ending of their personality – their self. For some there is the comfort of the idea of life after death; others believe that death is extinction.

Whether or not you believe in some kind of continuance after death, you may find the following imagination exercise a way of getting things into perspective:

Exercise: As this is a fairly long visualization exer-cise, it would be useful to get a friend to read it to you slowly, or to tape it yourself so that you can re-lax and respond to the images:

Imagine that you are walking along a country lane. It is a fine day – not too hot or too cold; there is a gentle breeze and the sun is shining. Alongside the path you are following is a small stream and as you walk along you can hear the water running and you can see the sun sparkling on the water.

Imagine what it would be like to be the water – freely flowing over the small stones running along the course of the stream. Notice how your speed changes as you flow through the landscape; speeding up as you flow down a slope, slowing down again as the land flattens out.

Now you flow into a river and are joined by other small streams all moving in the same direction. As a river you are part of something much larger and you are flowing more slowly through the landscape. Maybe the outlook changes as you flow through cities and towns; big and small ships float on your surface.

You are conscious of flowing towards the sea and eventually become part of the ocean. You are no longer conscious of the boundaries of the river bank – you are part of the boundless ocean. Imagine yourself as part of the still deeps, calm and secure. Imagine yourself as a

*wave, gathering strength and breaking into white foam
then returning to the surface.*

*Now you gather yourself and become a huge wave; feel
your power and strength. You rise up to the sky and
break into droplets of foam. As one of the droplets of
moisture you are transported up into the sky, into a
cloud where you gather with other droplets.*

*As the cloud you travel over the landscape; you can see
the ocean, the river and the stream where you began.
You fall out of the cloud as a drop of rain into the
stream and so are ready to begin your journey again.*

This exercise is a way of seeing the circle of life completed.
Whether or not you believe in life after death, you are part of the
natural world – the natural cycle of birth and development. As
such you have a place and a purpose.

Here is an exercise which will help you consider your purpose
in life:

*Exercise: This is also a visualization and so you
can record it yourself or get someone to read it out
for you.*

*Start by getting comfortable, relaxing and breathing
deeply.*

*Imagine that you are in a museum. Go into each of the
rooms where there are objects of various types. You are
in no hurry so you stroll around looking at anything
that takes your fancy.*

*You see a flight of stairs and climb up to the next
floor. There are more rooms of exhibits and you continue
your exploration.*

*In the room you are exploring now, you notice a door
which is partially open. You move towards it and open it
fully. You see a staircase leading upwards. It is quite
small and dark and seems to lead to a rarely-visited
part of the museum.*

*You decide to climb the stairs and when you do, you
come to a closed door at the top.*

You open the door and step into the room. You are in a large room, flooded with light so that you are slightly blinded for a moment. As your eyes get used to the light, you see that the room is lined with shelves of books and you begin to browse along the shelves.

You notice that in the corner of the room there is a large old-fashioned leather armchair in which an old person is sitting. You realize that this person is extremely wise and knows the answer to any question you might ask.

This person says, 'I've been expecting you; what do you want to know? You ask, 'What is the purpose for which I was born?'

Listen to the answer; ask the wise person any questions that you wish and when the dialogue is finished bid the person goodbye.

Turn back through the room, down the staircase and out of the museum.

When you finish this exercise, as before write or draw a picture about it. These kind of exercises can help you contact your unconscious wisdom; whatever comes into your mind is a message from yourself.

Saying Goodbye

Since this chapter is about the completing of circles, it's appropriate to think about how we manage the death of those who are close to us.

The time after the death of a loved one is bound to be one of great distress and upheaval. Researchers and writers on the subject of bereavement describe various stages, the first of which most usually is shock. This is a time when the world may seem unreal and you go through the expected rituals in a mechanical or numb state. It is as if your body and mind are protecting you from the full pain of feeling the loss.

The next stage, though, is one of suffering grief. Maybe anger and rage at the one who has died or towards people who you feel are to blame. Sometimes there are feelings of guilt characterized by 'If only I'd . . .' and 'I just wish I had . . .' You can prepare for and lessen the pain of this stage by trying to leave as little unfinished business with the person as possible. If there are things you want to say, say them; if there are things you want to do, do them while the person is alive so that you don't have unnecessary regrets about unexpressed thoughts and feelings.

As in other phases of life, working through loss can be seen as a series of tasks. As each one is completed another step is made towards acceptance. The most important task you have is to find a way of letting the person go so that you can continue your journey through life. Letting someone go doesn't mean forgetting them. You will always have the experience of their having been in your life. Their influence will remain and your memories will always be part of you. You may be familiar with a quotation from the Greek philosopher, Epictetus who counsels us to remember that we have those we love for the appointed season; 'if you long for your friend, or your son, when you cannot have them, you are wishing for figs in winter'.

In completing the process of mourning you are aiming to acknowledge that this phase of your life is over. You will be able to move forward into a new life without the presence of this person. Your memories will be with you but not in control of you.

Maybe as you have been reading this section you have been thinking of someone dear to you who has died. Maybe you need to stop for a while and think about anything you need still to do with regard to completing your grieving. Here is a meditation, based on Patricia Davis's 'Meditation for a Dead Friend' which might help you through a difficult time. If there are other people grieving with you, you might come together and work through this mutually.

> *Exercise: Choose a time when you can be uninterrupted for a while. Take time to prepare the room perhaps arranging a vase of flowers, lighting a candle, burning scented oils and so on.*

> *Sit quietly (in a circle if there is a group of you). Spend a few minutes breathing calmly so that you can centre your energy.*

Feel the love that you had for the person and see it in your mind's eye as a white light. Make a mental picture of the dead person and hold it in your mind. Imagine that you can beam the light towards your loved one so that he or she is bathed in the light. See the person standing in the centre of this light.

If there is anything you feel you need or want to say take this opportunity to do so. You can speak the words out loud or keep them in your mind.

Acknowledge and express your feelings.

Say 'goodbye'.

See your dear one, bathed in the light of your love, move into the distance. Let him or her go slowly but surely.

As he or she is lost to view, hold the knowledge that your time together will never be lost. You are taking it with you for the next stage of your journey.

And Finally, What Are You Waiting For?

Old habits die hard. Making changes takes time and energy. There will be times when you are sure you have made it – and then times when you are equally sure you never will. Don't get discouraged if you find that you occasionally fail to handle things better. Every skill you have ever mastered has been learnt through the mistakes you made.

Remember when you learned to drive a car? Play an instrument? Bake a cake? Started a new job? I guess you discovered that there was no magic way of mastering these skills. You probably had to make a lot of mistakes before you felt even the tiniest bit confident.

It doesn't matter that there is no magic which will transform you into a more successful time manager because magic is not necessary. You only need the will and the commitment. If you've got this far with the book and have had a go at most of the exercises, you've certainly demonstrated both will and commitment.

Whenever you find that things are not going to plan, don't get disheartened. Don't accept excuses from yourself like, 'I'm too tired/stupid/busy/old/young ...' Instead give yourself a treat for trying and then get back to thinking. Maybe you can see how you could have done things differently. Notice what you have learned from this experience and make a plan for next time.

Being in control of your time means having the freedom to choose alternatives. Remember that if what you are doing now does not work it is better to do something else rather than persisting with the thing that isn't working. You may not be able to make great changes in the outside world, but you can change how you think and how you make your decisions about what to do.

Don't waste any more time – what are you waiting for?

A Final Exercise

> *Imagine yourself in the role of a newspaper editor. The newspaper you edit is about you.*
>
> *Take a sheet of paper and decide on the title of the paper and design the heading. 'The Mary Johnson Times'/'Jim Ellison Chronicle' for example.*
>
> *Write down the date as it will be in three years' time and fill in the headlines as you would want them to be. 'Mary Makes It: University degree awarded to mother of four'; 'Jim Strikes Out On His Own: a new business started'; 'Ash-tray sales drop; "Smoking is a thing of the past for me" says successful former nicotine addict'.*
>
> *Keep this around so that you can continue to edit, update and so on. If you enjoy this, you could produce a weekly or monthly edition as a way of keeping yourself aware of the progress you are making.*

It's time now for me to finish. Go on and have the time of your life!

BOOKS USED AS
REFERENCES

Arroba, Tanya and James Kim, *Pressure at Work* McGraw Hill (UK) Ltd (1987)

Assagioli, Roberto, *Psychosynthesis* Turnstone Press (1974)

Berne, Eric, *Games People Play* Penguin Books (1968)

Berne, Eric, *What do you say when you've said Hello?* Corgi (1982)

Bettelheim, Bruno, *The Uses of Enchantment* Penguin Books (1976)

Dyer, Wayne, *Your Erroneous Zones* Sphere Books (1978)

Egan Gerard, *The Skilled Helper* Brooks/Cole, Monterey, California (1981)

Fisher, R and Ury, W, *Getting to Yes* Hutchinson (1983)

Friedman, M and Rosenbaum, R, *Type A Behaviour and Your Heart* Alfred A. Knopf (New York) 1974

James, John *The Game Plan* from *Transactional Analysis Journal* 3:4 (1973)

James, Muriel and Jongeward, Dorothy, *Born to Win* Addison-Wesley, Reading, Mass (1971)

Jeffers, Susan, *Feel the Fear and Do It Anyway* Century (1987)

Karpman, Stephen, *Fairy Tales and script drama analysis* from *Transactional Analysis Journal* 7:26 (1968)

Kubler-Ross, Elisabeth *On Death and Dying* Macmillan, New York (1969)

Leming, Michael and Dickinson, George, *Understanding Dying, Death and Bereavement* Holt Rinehart and Winston (1985)

Maslow, Abraham, *Toward a Psychology of Being* Van Nostrand (1962)

Selye, Hans, *The Stress of Life* McGraw-Hill, New York (1978)
Schwab, Johanna et al, *The Satir Approach to Communication* Science & Behaviour Books (1989)
Sheehy, G, *Passages* E. P. Dutton, New York, (1974)
Smith, Manuel, *When I Say No, I Feel Guilty*, Dial (1975)
Spitz, Renee, *Hospitalism: Genesis of Psychiatric Conditions in Early Childhood* published in *Psychoanalytic Study of the Child* 1: 53-74 (1945)
Steiner, Claude, *The Other Side of Power* Grove Press (1981)
Steiner, Claude, *Scripts People Live* Grove Press (1974)
Stevens, John O., *Awareness: exploring, experimenting, experiencing* Real People Press (1971)
Steward, Ian and Joines Vann, *TA Today* Lifespace Publishing (1987)